Modern Critical Interpretations

André Malraux's

Man's Fate

Modern Critical Interpretations

These and other titles in preparation

André Malraux's
Man's Fate

Edited and with an introduction by

Harold Bloom
Sterling Professor of the Humanities
Yale University

Chelsea House Publishers ◇ *1988*
NEW YORK ◇ NEW HAVEN ◇ PHILADELPHIA

© 1988 by Chelsea House Publishers, a division
of Chelsea House Educational Communications, Inc.
  95 Madison Avenue, New York, NY 10016
  345 Whitney Avenue, New Haven, CT 06511
  5068B West Chester Pike, Edgemont, PA 19028

Introduction © 1988 by Harold Bloom

Printed and bound in the United States of America

10 9 8 7 6 5 4 3 2 1

∞ The paper used in this publication meets the minimum
requirements of the American National Standard for
Permanence of Paper for Printed Library Materials,
Z39.48-1984.

Library of Congress Cataloging-in-Publication Data
André Malraux's Man's fate.
   (Modern critical interpretations)
   Bibliography: p.
   Includes index.
   Summary: A collection of critical essays on Malraux's novel
"Man's Fate" arranged in chronological order of publication.
   1. Malraux, André, 1901–1976.   Condition humaine.
2. China in literature. [1. Malraux, André, 1901–1976.
Man's fate.   2. French literature—History and criticism]
I. Bloom, Harold.   II. Series.
PQ2625.A716C583   1988   843'.912   87–20841
ISBN 1–55546–072–0 (alk. paper)

Contents

Editor's Note

This book brings together a representative selection of the best critical interpretations of André Malraux's major novel, *Man's Fate* (*La Condition humaine,* 1933). The critical essays are reprinted here in the chronological order of their original publication. All passages in French have been left untranslated where the critics have chosen to leave them so. I am grateful to Rhonda Garelick and Frank Menchaca for their assistance in editing this volume.

My introduction reads *Man's Fate* in terms of its heroes' sense of revolutionary belatedness, and interprets their fictive anxiety as a trope for Malraux's own aesthetic belatedness in regard to Dostoevsky and Conrad, his strong precursors. Geoffrey Hartman begins the chronological sequence with a meditation upon the process in which the heroes of *Man's Fate* must confront a final solitude, without ceasing to impose their wills upon the world.

In another study of "the Bolshevik hero" in the novel, David Wilkinson sees this mythic figure as "a Malrauvian, not a Marxist, breed." The Structuralist sociologist Lucien Goldmann finds that the laws and values that govern *Man's Fate* are those of "the revolutionary community," rather than those of the hero's individual realization.

Kyo is the focus of C. J. Greshoff's discussion of the gift of love in the novel, while LeRoy C. Breunig's brief essay traces changes in *Man's Fate*'s historical reception. The ethos of action in *Man's Fate* is seen by Derek W. Allan as Malraux's determination to accept, rather than escape, the human condition. W. M. Frohock, addressing the same issue, centers upon Gisors, finding in him an embodiment of Malraux's antihistoricism.

In this book's final essay, Roger Dial sees *Man's Fate* as a successful, but only momentary, fusion of Malraux's aesthetic heroism and Marxist ideals of the sacrifice of the individual to historical dialectics. I doubt the fusion, even in *Man's Fate,* and urge again the counterargument of my introduction, where the heroism of the belated revolutionary is defined in more aesthetic and Conradian terms.

Introduction

La Condition humaine (1933, known in English as *Man's Fate*) is judged universally to have been André Malraux's major novel. Rereading it in 1987, sixty years after the Shanghai insurrection of 1927, which it commemorates, is a rather ambiguous experience. One need not have feared that it would seem a mere period piece; it is an achieved tragedy, with the aesthetic dignity that the genre demands. What renders it a little disappointing is its excessive abstractness. Malraux may have known a touch too clearly exactly what he was doing. Rereading Faulkner always surprises; there is frequently a grace beyond the reach of art. Malraux's fictive economy is admirable, but the results are somewhat schematic. Clarity can be a novelistic virtue; transparency grieves us with the impression of a certain thin quality.

The idealistic revolutionaries are persuasive enough in *Man's Fate;* they are even exemplary. But, like all of Malraux's protagonists, they are diminished by their sense of *coming after their inspirers;* they are not forerunners, but belated imitators of the Revolution. Malraux's protagonists designedly quest for strength by confronting death, thus achieving different degrees either of communion or of solitude. Their models in fiction are the obsessed beings of Dostoevsky or of Conrad. *Man's Fate* cannot sustain comparison with *Nostromo,* let alone with the anguished narratives of Dostoevsky. There are no originals in Malraux, no strong revolutionaries who are the equivalents of strong poets, rather than of philosophers. Geoffrey Hartman, defending Malraux's stature as tragedian, sees the heroes of *Man's Fate* as understanding and humanizing the Nietzschean Eternal Recurrence:

> The tragic sentiment is evoked most purely not by multiplying lives . . . but by repeating the chances of death, of unique, fatal acts. A hero like Tchen, or his fellow conspirators Kyo and Katov, dies more than once.

1

But is that the Nietzschean issue, the Nietzschean test for strength? Do Malraux's heroes take on what Richard Rorty, following Nietzsche, has called "the contingency of selfhood"? Do they fully appreciate their own contingency? Here is Rorty's summary of this crucial aspect of Nietzsche's perspectivism:

> His perspectivism amounted to the claim that the universe had no lading-list to be known, of determinate length. He hoped that, once we realized that Plato's "true world" was just a fable, we would seek consolation, at the moment of death, not in having transcended the animal condition but in being that peculiar sort of dying animal who, by describing himself in his own terms, had created himself.

Nietzsche understood that political revolutionaries are more like philosophers than like poets, since revolutionaries also insist that the human condition bears only one true analysis. Malraux's heroes attempt to escape from contingency rather than, like the strong poets, accepting and then appropriating contingency. Though the heroes of *Man's Fate,* and of Malraux's other novels, meditate endlessly upon death, if only in order to achieve a sense of being, they never succeed in describing themselves entirely in their own terms. This is a clue to Malraux's ultimate inadequacy as a novelist, his failure to join himself to the great masters of French fiction: Stendhal, Balzac, Flaubert, Proust, or to the international novelists he most admired: Dostoevsky, Conrad, Faulkner. Would we say of the protagonists of Stendhal and Balzac that the death which overcomes them "is no more than the symbol of an ultimate self-estrangement"? Hartman's remark is valid for Malraux's heroes, but not for Stendhal's or Balzac's.

Malraux, a superb and wary critic, defended himself against Gaëtan Picon's shrewd observation that: "Malraux, unlike Balzac or Proust, in no way seeks to give each character a personal voice, to free each character from its creator." His response was: "The autonomy of characters, the particular vocabulary given to each of them are powerful techniques of fictional action; they are not necessities . . . I do not believe that the novelist must create *characters;* he must create a particular and coherent world." *Man's Fate* certainly does create such a world; is it a liability or not that Kyo, Katov, Gisors and the others fall short as characters, since they do not stride out of the novel, breaking loose from Malraux, and they all of them do sound rather alike. I finish rereading *Nostromo,* and I brood on the flamboyant Capataz, or I put down *As I Lay Dying,* and Darl Bundren's very individual voice haunts me. But Kyo and Katov give me nothing to meditate upon, and Gisors and Ferral speak with the same inflection and vocabulary. Fate or contingency resists appropriation by Malraux's heroes, none of whom defies, or breaks free of, his creator.

Despite Malraux's defense, the sameness of his protagonists constitutes a definite aesthetic limitation. It would be one thing to create varied individuals with unique voices and then to show that they cannot communicate with one another. It is quite another thing to represent so many aspects of the author as so many characters, all speaking with his voice, and then demonstrate the deathliness of their inability to speak truly to another. Malraux confused death with contingency, which is a philosopher's error, rather than a strong novelist's.

This may be why the women throughout Malraux's novels are so dismal a failure in representation. Unamuno ironically jested that "all women are one woman," which is just the way things are in Malraux's fictions. A novelist so intent upon Man rather than men is unlikely to give us an infinite variety of women.

What redeems Man's Fate from a reader's frustration with the sameness of its characters is the novel's indubitable capture of a tragic sense of life. Tragedy is not individual in Malraux, but societal and cultural, particularly the latter. Malraux's Marxism was always superficial, and his aestheticism fortunately profound. The tragedy of the heroes in Man's Fate is necessarily belated tragedy, which is fitting for idealists whose place in revolutionary history is so late. That is why Gisors is shown teaching his students that: "Marxism is not a doctrine, it is a *will* . . . it is the will to know themselves . . . to conquer without betraying yourselves." Just as the imagination cannot be distinguished from the will as an artistic tradition grows older and longer, so ideology blends into the will as revolutionary tradition enters a very late phase. Tragedy is an affair of the will, and not of doctrine. Kyo and Katov die in the will, and so achieve tragic dignity. Gisors, the best mind in the novel, sums up for Malraux, just a few pages from the end:

> She was silent for a moment:
> "They are dead, now," she said finally.
> "I still think so, May. It's something else. . . . Kyo's death is not only grief, not only change—it is . . . a metamorphosis. I have never loved the world over-much: it was Kyo who attached me to men, it was through him that they existed for me. . . . I don't want to go to Moscow. I would teach wretchedly there. Marxism has ceased to live in me. In Kyo's eyes it was a will, wasn't it? But in mine, it is a fatality, and I found myself in

harmony with it because my fear of death was in harmony with fatality. There is hardly any fear left in me, May; since Kyo died, I am indifferent to death. I am freed (freed! . . .) both from death and from life. What would I do over there?"

"Change anew, perhaps."

"I have no other son to lose."

The distinction between a will and a fatality is the difference between son and father, activist and theoretician, latecomer and forerunner. For Malraux, it is an aesthetic distinction, rather than a psychological or spiritual difference. As novelist, Malraux takes no side in this dichotomy, an impartiality at once his narrative strength and his representational weakness. He gives us forces and events, where we hope for more, for access to consciousnesses other than our own, or even his. As a theorist of art, Malraux brilliantly grasped contingency, but as a novelist he suffered it. He saw that the creator had to create his own language out of the language of precursors, but he could not enact what he saw. *Man's Fate* is a memorable tragedy without memorable persons. Perhaps it survives as a testament of Malraux's own tragedy, as a creator.

"The Silence of the Infinite Spaces"

Geoffrey H. Hartman

Malraux entitles his . . . greatest novel *La Condition humaine*. Political in subject, it is, like *The Conquerors*, more than political in range, and deepens the definition of Man explored in the previous books. Of the novel's seven chapters, the first two tell of the quick success of the Shanghai insurrection, while the remainder portray an ironical, protracted series of events, reducing the characters one by one to solitude. Because, in the first part of the story, they can still impose their world on the world, they also succeed in imposing their will. Yet, from the outset, a contrary pattern prevails, ripened by apparently external circumstances. Soon every character suffers an experience of self-estrangement through which he becomes aware of the radical gap between the world and his view of it. A moment of "the silence of the infinite spaces" mocks his deepest dreams, and, though it may not alter his will to act, suggests a contradiction, inescapable in its nature, between Man and History.

In this book Malraux's architectonic vigour surpasses any shown before; it almost convinces us that the form of the novel is the natural medium for his view of life. The premise that Man inevitably imposes his world on the world, that thought and act are fictional in essence, grants the slightest event the same expressive potential as the greatest. It is true, at least, that Malraux's power of *development* has advanced. We can take, as an example, his treatment of what was probably the germinal incident of the novel. Towards the end of the *Psychology of Art* he remarks:

From *André Malraux*. © 1960 by Geoffrey H. Hartman. Hilary House Publishers, 1960.

> Every man's self is a tissue of fantastic dreams. I have written
> elsewhere of the man who fails to recognize his own voice on
> the gramophone . . . and because our throat alone transmits to
> us our inner voice I named the book *La Condition Humaine*. In
> art the other voices do but ensure the transmission of this inner
> voice. The artist's message owes its force to the fact that it arises
> from the heart of silence, from a devastating loneliness that
> conjures up the universe so as to impose on it a human accent.

The incident to which the author refers occupies an unobtrusive section
at the beginning of the novel. Kyo is listening to records prepared by the
conspirators, which purport to teach a foreign language but actually transmit secret messages. Kyo, who does not recognize his own voice in recorded
form, thinks the disks have been changed or that the phonograph distorts,
but the matter is quickly dropped. Malraux allows the event to interpret
itself by haunting the consciousness of Kyo, who associates more and more
persons with it. When, for example, he tells his father (Gisors) about the
estranged voice, the latter explains: "We hear the voices of others with our
ears, our own voice with our throat." And he adds, astonishingly: "Opium
is also a world we do not hear with our ears." Thus one germinal detail
gathers momentum and begins to symbolize the human condition in its
entirety. Gisors himself takes opium, and it seems that every man, wittingly
or unwittingly, finds a way to overcome an irreducible solitude. The world
of Man's perceptions is, like that of the artist, a second birth, a world
conjured up to impose on it a specifically human accent.

As with the detail so with the persons. There are many characters now,
none really minor, and all affected in various ways by a radical experience
of estrangement. Kyo fails to recognize *his* voice; Tchen did not recognize
his arm. Some, like Gisors, are always aware of an inner desolation; others,
like Kyo, the man of action, who distrusts his father's tendency to convert
every experience to knowledge, only by usurpation or chance. The death
which overcomes Malraux's heroes is no more than the symbol of an
ultimate self-estrangement. And even those who survive do not always
escape it.

Malraux is, at last, in full possession of his idea. He has found a law
encompassing all "fatality," and can give each of his characters an individual
and widely varying fate because they are still instances of that law. Man,
as *The Royal Way* had implied, is defined by the world he imposes on the
world, not potentially but actually. Man's fate, the present novel adds,
follows from his nature. What is *fate* except an inextricable involvement

with the world, one which comes about because of the nature of Man, who wants to make the world inseparable from his life?

That this attempt, however vital, must fail, is the *condition humaine* out of which Man's greatness and tragedy spring. Malraux stands close to the existentialistic thesis that we "invent" our fate in order to be irremediably bound to the world. But even though every such "invention" reveals a specific power in Man to impose his world on the world, it is also an escape from his intrinsic solitude, and leaves an anguish that tells he is greater than the sum of his acts.

The multiplication of individual destinies is also part of a more relaxed and "epical" narrative manner. Tchen still runs to his fate as if action were a drug against solitude which wears off and had to be increased. But others move at different speeds, and reach their fulfilment at different points in the plot, which is no longer in a state of continuous high tension. The specifically *literary* problem which Malraux solves in the present novel is how to convey Man's pursuit of fate without the artificial, fantastic tempo of *The Conquerors* or the conglomeration of synthetically staged adventures we find in *The Royal Way*. His problem is of the same order as that of an artist who strives to obtain a three-dimensional effect with two-dimensional means, to show that the medium does not have to be of the same nature as the thing it represents. All problems of this order are essentially aesthetic and imply that artistic freedom consists in the power to represent an experience without being subject to its law.

If we compare two incidents, of how man runs towards his fate, one from *La Condition humaine* and the other from *The Conquerors*, Malraux's new artistic freedom will appear in greater relief. In the latter, Klein, a friend of Garine's and fellow-worker in the strike, is taken hostage by the terrorists and killed. Garine and the narrator are told that a number of bodies have been found and go to identify them. As a morbid joke the terrorists have propped the bodies upright, and for once the narrator's speed of perception fails: "As soon as I raise my eyes I see the four bodies, *standing*." The author here suggests two things: an event too quick for human eyes, and that Klein's body *is* death, as if death had been within him as a hidden fatality. The slashes on Klein's face, perceived later, express a further trick of fate: Klein was always terrified at the idea of knife-killings. Then Garine wants to close his comrade's eyes, and, with a blindly foreseeing gesture, puts two fingers "stretched apart like scissors" on the white eyeballs—realizes the murderers have cut the eyelids off.

The scene described above is one of the finest in *The Conquerors*. It haunts the mind by its compression and its obsessive emphasis on the faculty of sight. It seeks to show that fate is quicker than Man, and yet within Man, who anticipates and even conspires with its action. A very different scene, expressing the same idea, occurs just before Kyo listens to his voice and does not recognize it. Very casual, it is enlivened by a single naïve gesture. Tchen has just informed his comrades of the completed murder, and feels a great need to leave them and confide in Gisors, because no one else, except perhaps Katov, is really close to him:

> The Russian [Katov] was eating little sugar candies, one by one without taking his eyes off Tchen who suddenly understood the meaning of gluttony. Now that he had killed he had the right to crave anything he wished. The right. Even if it were childish. He held out his square hand. Katov thought he wanted to leave and shook it. Tchen got up. It was just as well: he had nothing more to do here; Kyo was informed, it was up to him to act. As for himself, he knew what he wanted to do now. He reached the door, returned however.
> "Pass me the candy."
> Katov gave him the bag. He wanted to divide the contents: no paper. He filled his cupped hand, chewed with his whole mouth, and went out.
> "Shouldn't 've gone 'lone," said Katov.
> A refugee in Switzerland from 1905 to 1912, date of his clandestine return to Russia, he spoke French almost without accent, but he swallowed certain of his vowels, as though to compensate for the necessity of articulating carefully when he spoke Chinese. Almost directly under the lamp, very little light fell on his face. Kyo preferred this: the expression of ironic ingenuousness which the small eyes and especially the upturned nose (a sly sparrow, said Hemmelrich) gave to Katov's face, struck him all the more as it jarred with his own features and often troubled him.
> "Let's get it over with," said Kyo. "You have the records, Lou?"

The passage effects a transition from one personal focus to another, from Tchen to Kyo. In so doing it swiftly illuminates the relationship between both and the third main character, Katov. Though the latter is a pivot he appears momentarily in greatest relief: his personality is an *unknown* which Tchen and Kyo (and Hemmelrich) cannot solve. Katov is often kept opaque, and he does not hold the centre until the last great scene of his sacrifice and death. Still, we are often shown into his thoughts, and if he remains mysterious here it is because Malraux always chooses some opaque pivot around which actions or thoughts turn. In Tchen's first scene it is the victim shrouded by the white gauze; in Katov's last scene the strangely empty space of the prison compound; and often such an obscure experience as that which Tchen wishes to clarify with Gisor's help, or that which Kyo puzzles over after hearing his voice in recorded form.

Malraux's characters are defined by their different reaction to this "unknown." All are drawn towards it like Perken to the idea of torture, or Claude to his map, or the conquerors to "China." But now Malraux varies more skilfully the structure of each fascination, its momentum, form and quality. Both Tchen and Kyo subtly transform the other man, make him less strange, more at one with their wishes. The manner in which each imposes his world on the world is, however, quite different.

Tchen is strongly conscious of his solitude, his increased familiarity with death, and wants to deny it. He thinks he understands Katov's "gluttony," but when the latter misinterprets his outstretched hand, we are reminded of the distance between any gesture and its interpretation, as well as of the distance between Katov and Tchen which the latter would have liked to deny. Yet Tchen accepts Katov's misunderstanding too quickly, and his returning for the candy, and gulping all of it, has something equally hasty about it, this time wilful rather than spontaneous. It may reflect the speed with which he moves towards his "fate." As for Kyo, he tends to pass over differences in character, proceeding by the quickest route to the next item: "Let's get it over with." He too, therefore, displays a certain haste. Katov, finally, appears kind and relaxed, but there is the suggestion of gluttony and that curious "swallowing of vowels." The whole scene has a great deal of humorous strength not found in any of Malraux's previous work except his fantasies.

The estrangements of which we have talked always occur in the midst of the secret haste the above passage hints at. When the records are played, Kyo hears a voice he does not recognize as his own. Despite the fraternal effort of revolution, all the characters, by the end of the novel, come to face death or destiny alone, strangers to themselves and to the world. The moment of death is, in fact, associated with this leitmotif of the strange voice. Just before Kyo joins Katov in the prisoner compound and takes poison, he passes through an experience in which it plays a deeply disguised role.

König, Chiang Kai-shek's police chief, in charge of rooting out the Communist revolutionaries, has heard that Kyo is a believer in the "dignity of Man." He therefore has Kyo brought from prison and plans to make him betray his belief. During their interview the telephone rings and a voice asks whether Kyo is *still* alive. Soon it rings a second time with, apparently, the same query. König, in the meantime, has begun an aimless interrogation. Does Kyo want to live? Is Kyo a Communist through . . . dignity? Kyo, who does not see a purpose to these questions, tensely expects the telephone: when it rings a third time König lets it ring, hand on receiver, asking where the Communists have hidden their arms—another pointless question, since he already knows the answer or does not need Kyo for it. Then, suddenly, Kyo understands that the telephone is merely a piece of stage-business.

What business Malraux does not say, but König is obviously not interested in specific information. He wants merely the gesture of betrayal, and later offers Kyo his freedom in exchange for it. The business of the telephone, a devilish variant on the game of one two three . . . gone, is rigged up to achieve this end. For the repeated ring suggests more than a limit to Kyo's life which König (the name perhaps symbolic) has the power to suspend. It evokes the *indifference* of the world—that repetitive machine, that strange anonymous voice—to Man's existence and will. The real temptation faced by Kyo is not König's power or his humane offer but the subtler suggestion of this voice. It demands nothing except the sacrifice of an idea, the idea of Man. The inhuman whistle of the locomotive which later pierces the prisoner compound, the scene of Kyo's and Katov's death, is the image of König's telephone raised to the height of impotent terror.

The tragedy Malraux depicts, and which the world of *Man's Fate* embodies most clearly, does not stem from any special flaw in the protagonists. It comes, at first sight, from the brutal confrontation of Man with external fate. Yet each of the novels shows a reversal in which external forms of fate appear as invited or even invented by Man. A later work such as *Man's Hope,* in which the author feels even freer towards his idea, suggests this reversal also in occasional images, as when Loyalist aeroplanes appear to *seek* the enemy's anti-aircraft fire. Malraux's view should, however, be distinguished from religious and psychological concepts of fate. The former may hold that a person creates what he deserves, the latter that he creates for himself what he most deeply wants or is compelled to want because of early experiences. For Malraux there is a fatality prior to every individual fate, and this lies in the specific nature of Man, who cannot accept a world independent of his act, and so aspires to identify himself with forces greater than his being, even at the risk of losing part of his humanity. This risk is expressed in the general theme of self-estrangement, as well as by the symbols of alienated or inhuman face and voice. König with his telephone and the atrocious whistle of the locomotive has donned the mask of fate: he is assimilated to what has crushed him and propagates its horror compulsively. But the tragic, rather than demonic, figures show their greatest strength as they stand alone, betrayed by the forces they have called up, deeply conscious of their power not to be seduced. Katov and Kyo wear their own faces and speak with their own voice.

The Bolshevik Hero

David Wilkinson

Malraux's next two novels [*Man's Fate* and *Days of Wrath*], completed in
1933 and 1935 (at the height of his own period of cooperation with the
Communists), represent a distinct phase in his development. Not a party
member, he rejects both the organizational methods of the party and a key
aspect of Marxist dogma. But the central figures of *Man's Fate* and *Days of
Wrath* are Communists because in this period Malraux has accepted without
any reluctance the value of fighting the same fight as that of the Communists. *Man's Fate* arrives at this conclusion by debating what Malraux
sees as the alternative ways to lead one's life at a moment of revolutionary
crisis. *Days of Wrath* dispenses with the debate entirely. Both works present
mythic, exemplary heroes—figures not to be rejected, like those of the
preceding works, but worthy of imitation. Malraux has reached his first
resting point here, his first partly stable notion of what is man's political
good. This abstract idea of the good life is rendered concrete in the successful
lives of Kyo Gisors and Kassner, in the successful figure of the Bolshevik
hero.

    Man's Fate (1933) appears to employ a plot structure familiar to Mal-
raux: action, apparent success, failure. But at the opening of *Man's Fate,* as
if to differentiate it from the works that come before, stands not a journey
but a murder. At the end, there is not death or departure but a succession,
a new and yet renewed debate, a continuation into the future. If the future
has ever until now had any meaning or real existence for Malraux, his

From *Malraux: An Essay in Political Criticism.* © 1967 by the President and Fellows
of Harvard College. Harvard University Press, 1967.

readers have not been made aware of it. With all its similarities, real and apparent, to its predecessors, *Man's Fate* is a different book. Still an enormous exploration and lesson in the tragic shape of human destiny, it constitutes a new lesson, breaking new ground.

The plot is more complex than earlier ones (though this point is not significant for the present investigation), and the action will demand and accept the summary of "success and later failure." The greater complexity simply consists of the larger involvement of those characters other than the central figure in the movement of the novel; more attention must be directed to them; and this orientation becomes the ostensible reason for a more basic search into these other figures than the highly concentrated focus of *The Conquerors* permitted. The time is March 1927, the place Shanghai. The Kuomintang, which now holds Hankow as well as Canton, is moving northward over the hopeless opposition of various forces; those that matter briefly in the novel are the "White" forces associated with the Shanghai government. The immediate issue is over the seizure of Shanghai—will it fall to the organized Communist groups within or to the "Blue" Nationalist army of Chiang Kai-shek? For Chiang is on the verge of splitting with the Communists, until now his allies in the Kuomintang, and the question of who takes Shanghai points beyond itself to the question of which will be victorious in China in the struggle which both know must come. More to the reader's interest are the problematic relation between the hierarchical Communist party (centered now in Hankow) and the Shanghai revolutionaries (who are still psychological individualists, if individualist in no other way) and the general relation between order and the person in a situation of revolt. And, inevitably, the destiny of men, taken one after the other, as a clue to the destiny of man.

A Communist insurrection, led by Kyo Gisors and the Russian Katov, captures Shanghai in about a day and a half. The Communists divert a government arms shipment to themselves and by distributing the weapons turn a general strike into a revolution. The Shanghai Communists have won, Chiang is forestalled. But already in the first day of the uprising preparations are being made by the president of the French Chamber of Commerce, Ferral, to deal with Chiang Kai-shek and to turn him against the Communists. As the city falls, the deal is closed; and one portion of the action ends with the presentation to the Communists of a Blue order to surrender their arms and leave themselves helpless. Kyo and his friend Ch'en, a terrorist, make a journey to Hankow, trying and failing to receive the support of the International in a refusal to give up their weapons and an immediate break with Chiang. Ch'en returns, to be killed in an unsuccessful attempt on Chiang's life. Kyo also returns, to organize combat groups and await the inevitable repression. When it comes, he is arrested and later commits suicide; Katov is taken and executed, along with all the other revolutionaries except for a few who escape to continue the fight or to muse upon it. The plot itself, like that of *The Royal Way,* ends in a defeat. But an analysis of the characters individually leads to a different "conclusion."

The apparently stable plot is dominated by the new method of constructing the actual argument. Instead of examining the life of one moral prototype, finding the elements of strength and weakness in that type, the reader is exposed to a large set of important characters. Each of them displays a certain perception of the Absurd and a certain reaction to it: all are figures searching for some enduring value in the face of isolation, defeat, and death. Though they do not argue the case for the lives they lead with as many words as do the figures of *Man's Hope, Man's Fate* is nevertheless a debate among many possible responses to the Absurd—a debate in which the characters argue with their lives.

The point at issue is the response of the hero to his predicament. Each character becomes aware of a particular mask of the Absurd, a manifestation of destiny which stands in his path. How does he react to it? Does he attempt to blind himself to its existence? Does he submit to it and become an instrument? Does he revolt against it, attempt to conquer it, and turn it to use? And is his conquest merely a pretense, the verbal screen for a hidden surrender or a real failure? To this interrogation the figures of this political novel must be subjected, to discover which of them, if any, is indeed its hero.

Each key figure has his own special ordeal. König, Chiang Kai-shek's police chief, cannot forget that once, when he was captured and tortured by the Reds in Russia, he wept before them; now he is forever obsessed by that memory, driven literally to lose himself, unable to forget his disgust with himself and his humiliation, unable ever to recapture what he was. The Baron de Clappique has fallen out of his social place into a sordid subterranean life on the fringes of the night world of Shanghai; he cannot think of his degradation without renewed anguish. Old Gisors, Kyo's father, is an intellectual, anguished for a more Malrauvian reason: the constant perception of his own solitude, the fear of death. Ferral, president of the Franco-Asiatic consortium and the French Chamber of Commerce, in terror of being dependent upon the will of another, is beset by the craving for power and the fear that it will escape him. The phonograph seller Hemmelrich, who has lived an atrocious life of poverty and wretchedness for thirty-seven years, writhes at the thought of a future like his past, in which he cannot afford to die because he has a family but cannot alleviate the misery of his wife or the constant pain of his sick child. The young Westernized Chinese, Ch'en, has received from a Lutheran pastor a deep religious anxiety, an agony of sin and shame, a consciousness of isolation from the world, a need to fulfill an apostleship—but no love, no religious vocation, no faith. This variety of human torment is in sharp contrast to the morbid unity of Perken's obsession: some of these maladies look superficially more curable than the consciousness of death. But in fact it is mainly those who are doomed to die who make the best of life, those who want something from life who live on contemptibly and in despair.

The responses to the human lot in *Man's Fate* fall into three broad groups: some men, like the Conquerors, seek their defense in power and violence; others seek to escape by transforming their consciousness, overcoming their perceptions of the world; still others are revolutionaries who find the causes of their condition in the social order and attempt to amend it.

König, Ch'en, and Ferral belong to the first group. König's memory of humiliation by torture can be wiped away, for a moment only, by torture and murder, by the killing of a whole class of men whom he holds responsible. He was tortured by the Reds: now "*my* dignity is to kill them"; he believes that he can live the life of a man again only when he feeds his solitude with blood. And even to kill is not enough—first he must degrade and humiliate the victim just as he has been degraded. He is exacting retribution, but not retribution alone. König denies that he is a free man, free to choose his own way of living. Because the Reds drove nails into his shoulders, and because he wept before them, he lives by punishing them; because he insists on blood, he must not admit to himself that he could have lived otherwise. Only if he can persuade his victim to degrade himself—as had König—during the ordeal can he prove—as he must prove again and again—that men with a dignity of their own do not exist. If no one can withstand his torture, then dignity consists merely in being torturer rather than victim, and König possesses all that life can afford a man; if no one can withstand his torture, then the humiliated cannot choose their lives, and König could not have chosen to become anything but what he is. His justification of and satisfaction from his life require a certain submission from all his prisoners. König captures the revolutionary Kyo Gisors, converses with him humanely, hears him talk of his decision for the revolution as the product of "a will to dignity." König determines to pull him down, as he must. He interrogates Kyo; he cajoles him, threatens him, tempts him to change sides and save his life; "only I will know it"—know again, that is, that men in torment are *all* without dignity. Kyo refuses and is sent to be killed. König has not had his full measure of satisfaction: his solution to the problem of his own pain has been violated, for he has only captured the body of his victim. Worse still than this outrage is the fact that a man should have endured the same atrocious condition that distorted and destroyed König: for now König can know that it was not his condition but his choice of a cure for it that deformed him as a man and made his loss of dignity permanent. He might have recovered himself, but his defense was both unworthy and unsuccessful.

By the time König comes onstage, the independent elements of his personality have long since vanished and he has been swallowed up by his role: counterrevolutionary in politics, policeman in society, killer in existential reality. Ch'en Ta-erh is swallowed up before our eyes by the role of anarchist assassin, terrorist, Conqueror and murderer. He appears first as a revolutionary conspirator who stabs a sleeping man as a matter of duty; he dies in political and actual solitude as a man who has parted with revolution in order to make terrorism into the meaning of his life. To possess himself he must become a lonely executioner. Killing—political killing of certain men, as for König—is what will free him from his absurd burden.

The Absurd presents itself to Ch'en as religious angst without the comforts of religion. Like the pastor, his teacher, Ch'en is driven to forget himself in action, to justify his life by making a sacrifice of it. But Ch'en's religious version of the unhappy consciousness lacks the charity that might direct him to sacrifice for others, and it lacks the inner life and sense of the presence of the divine that might permit a religious renunciation: since he has no faith, religion cannot be his defense. He is seduced away from Pastor Smithson by an intellectual recruiter for the revolution, who plays on his illusion of heroism to bring him into political activity.

In the course of this activity Ch'en becomes a decisive influence, setting off both the revolt and the repression. To him this is only by the way, for he is entirely involved with the meaning of his acts for himself, for his own life. He begins by murdering a man so as to steal a paper which will get the insurrection the arms it must have to start. But for him the political meaning of the act vanishes as it is performed and is replaced by an entirely personal, religious one. He feels that the murder has thrown him into a world from which there will be no escape. By his bloody act he is in his own mind set apart from "men who do not kill," cut off from the realm of the living, absorbed into a world of murder, of imprisoning solitude and increasing anguish. He struggles to return, but he cannot. Neither in conversation nor in action can he convey what he has felt, his sudden familiarity with death. As his combat group attacks a police station, they link arms in a chain on its roof (the top man holding to a roof ornament so that the bottom man can hurl grenades through a window): "In spite of the intimacy of death, in spite of that fraternal weight which was pulling him apart, he was not one of them." The murder means, to him, the revelation and the seal on his utter solitude.

But this world of solitude that he has discovered is created by a specific act and can only enfold him completely when he repeats that act. Ch'en becomes obsessed with the idea of terrorism. His sleep is poisoned with new anguish, with terrible monsters conjured from his memories of murder, that only a new plan and a new murder will relieve. He begins to draw away from the other revolutionaries, to defy discipline as well as doctrine, to insist upon the assassination of Chiang Kai-shek. He breaks with them and makes an attempt on Chiang's life.

Politically this is the provocation that sparks the repression. For Ch'en the decision to kill has (again) a personal meaning only. He tries to give it a political meaning as well by fabricating an ideology of terrorism: the individual without hope, says this ideology, must find an immediate meaning to his life, not through an organization, but through an idea—the idea of martyrdom; the terrorist mystique will require every man in solitude to assume a responsibility, to appoint himself the judge of an oppressor's life, to decide alone, to execute alone, and to die alone. But this mystique is without political end, is intended to achieve nothing beyond the deaths of the "accused" and his "judge." The only meaning available to the individual is, therefore, the immediate meaning: he kills; he dies. Ch'en makes no serious attempt to convey this mystique to others or to judge whether or not Chiang or some other should be killed. An ideology which cannot survive its author has a merely personal meaning. The decision to make an attempt in which he must die silences Ch'en's nagging anguish and replaces it with a "radiant exaltation," a complete possession of himself. Thus it appears that his true object is in his own death, met amid a ritual of sacrifice. He achieves his objective.

Ch'en's reaction to his "human condition" has in common with those of the other Conquerors, which otherwise it hardly resembles, that it takes the form of a sickness, and of a submersion in sickness, rather than a cure. His self-destruction does not even pretend to free him. His world, so alien to that of men, is finally dominated, not by men, but by death and by fatality. Yet on one occasion it seems to Kyo that Ch'en embodies man himself, a moth that creates the very light in which he will destroy himself.

No argument in *Man's Fate* denies it: only the lives, and even more the deaths, of Katov and of Kyo himself.

The entrepreneur Ferral, the third of the Conqueror-types in *Man's Fate,* is what Garine might have become by living to associate himself with England. Ferral is an ex-intellectual and former deputy, using his enterprises in the Orient as the stairway back to power in France. The revolution menaces the Chinese portions of his empire, and he reacts vigorously even while it is in progress, routing out the money which will enable Chiang to pay his army and break at once with the Communists. He is successful in buying off Chiang, but at the moment of success his financial troubles grow; though he has beaten the nearest enemy, he is in turn vanquished in his own field, and his consortium is finally dissolved.

Ferral is thoroughly devoted to power seeking. Intelligence for him is "the possession of the means of coercing things or men," and he thinks of other men not as persons, but as part of a network of mechanisms to be operated. " 'A man is the sum of his action, of what he has *done,* of what he can do. Nothing else. I am not what such and such an encounter with a man or woman may have done to shape my life; I am my roads.' " Yet he vaguely suspects how thoroughly dependent he is on forces which he does not control, and it is made inescapably plain to him when, after his victory, a roomful of candy-chewing "sedentary nonentities"—the representatives of the French banks—in a long, incomprehensible ritual deny him the funds needed to save the consortium and the power for which he has fought.

Old Gisors identifies Ferral's real urge, one that is both endless and hopeless.

> "Men are perhaps indifferent to real power . . . the king's power . . . the power to govern. . . . What fascinates them . . . is not real power, it's the illusion of being able to do exactly as they please. . . . Man has no urge to govern: he has an urge to compel . . . to be more than a man, in a world of men. To escape man's fate, I was saying. Not powerful: all-powerful. The visionary disease, of which the will to power is only the intellectual justification, is the will to god-head: every man dreams of being god."

Gisors also remarks that "there is always a need for intoxication: this country has opium . . . the West has woman. . . . Perhaps love is above all the means which the Occidental uses to free himself from man's fate." For Ferral, if we read "eroticism" for "love," this is true: his ideal "power" is really the complete sexual possession of a woman, and he carries out operations in that sphere in just the same manner as in those of counterrevolutionary and financial maneuvering, with the same absorption—in fact, with the same ending. This will to possess dominates his relation with his mistress, Valerie: by giving her sexual pleasure and by humiliating her, he believes, he triumphs over her. But this triumph is not lasting, for she responds by making him ridiculous in public; in turn, furious with humiliation, he imagines fantastic punishments, finally fills her rooms with animals and satisfies himself by humiliating a prostitute in his turn. "His will to power never achieved its object"; he could never possess another completely nor completely penetrate the consciousness of a woman; "in reality he never went to bed with anyone but himself." His activity is frenzied and meaningless, and a wash-drawing he has placed on his wall is his emblem: "on a discolored world over which travelers were wandering, two exactly similar skeletons were embracing each other in a trance." And to give the lie to all the activity which is only a disguise, there is his strange, superficially inappropriate craving for sleep:

> Sleep was peace. He had lived, fought, created; beneath all those appearances, deep down, he found this to be the only reality, the joy of abandoning himself, of leaving upon the shore, like the body of a drowned companion, that creature, himself, whose life it was necessary each day to invent anew. "To sleep is the only thing I have always really wanted, for so many years."

Games of power which defeat him, craving for an omnipotence which he can never reach, the need to inflict humiliations which end in his own humiliation, the need to possess and to possess what forever escapes him, a flight at last from himself into sleep where he finds only nightmares and, once more, himself: all are forms of the attempt to be released from "man's fate," and all, equally, fail.

Ferral and König each yield to an obsession growing out of past humiliation, Ch'en to one with which his mentor infects him. Each permits his obsession, with power or violence, to create an inner anxiety that is relieved only in the anticipation or the act of damaging, indirectly or directly, some other person. But the compulsion to rule, to torture, or to kill grows insatiable and boundless. They must fail to satisfy it sooner or later. But only Ch'en discovers the true end toward which the impossible desire points: permanent peace; self-destruction. In the earlier stages of this passage from obsession to death, Ferral and König (who leave their victims alive) no doubt transmit their disorders as Ch'en's pastor transmitted his own, for they present to others the same experience of humiliation that molded them. They are the carriers of the Absurd, as they are its victims. This latter quality at least they share with those who would defend themselves through changing their ways of looking at the world. If those who choose to be intoxicated with action destroy others as well as themselves, those who choose other forms of intoxication (that touch themselves only) are perhaps to be preferred. That they turn against themselves at least suggests that those who turned against society did so by choice rather than by necessity: that, despite the seeming logic of their lives, they could have done otherwise.

As Malraux continues to explore the question, "How can a man live?"—which is to say, how can one contend with one's human lot—he encounters answers that are as futile as they are fascinating. One answer that fascinates is the Baron de Clappique's: mythomania. Clappique is a fugitive, expatriate, penniless, fallen member of a deteriorated upper class. His normal existence is sordid: he is first found playing the fool in a jazz hall, the Black Cat, between a pair of dance girls. He appears simply whimsical, but he is like the other denizens of that fringe world, "in the depths of an identical despair." He drinks, throws away all his money in one night, concocts variegated and fabulous tales about himself, with one object: the denial of his life, of his decline. Wealth does not exist, poverty does not exist; " 'Nothing exists: all is dream.' " Kyo and his father have an occasion to discuss him: " 'No man exists by denying life.' . . . 'One lives inadequately by it. . . . He feels a need to live inadequately.' 'And he is forced to.' 'He chooses a way of life that *makes* it necessary.' " Old Gisors claims that Clappique's affliction has no more depth than the man himself; but if Clappique's is not deep, it is still the same malady that belongs to all men. He cannot think of the manner of life from which he has fallen without one form of anguish, and his simple confrontation with the serenity of the Japanese painter, Kama, brings him another: "the atrocious sensation of suffering in the presence of a creature who denied suffering."

Like the others Clappique senses the presence of an Absurd; he tries to defend himself against it by outperforming it in absurdity, by means of his fantastic vagaries. He suffers and denies it as best he can—though absurdity personified never thoroughly outfaces the Absurd even in his normal life—by making everything into an alcoholic or outrageous dream, even his own being: " 'Baron de Clappique does not exist.' "

Clappique becomes involved with the revolutionaries by chance, because he runs out of money and can be of some service to them in obtaining the arms shipment; the police, for whom he has usually provided information, discover this, and his connection with Kyo leads one of his contacts, on the day before the repression, to warn Clappique to leave Shanghai. Instead, Clappique warns Kyo; the latter, who has long since made up his mind to stay and fight to the end, asks Clappique to go back to try to obtain more information; Clappique arranges to meet him at the Black Cat. Before the appointment, with time to spare, Clappique is attracted to a gambling house; the information he has, vital to Kyo, is forgotten as Clappique suddenly seems to find himself in the world of true and unconcealed reality, a man confronted by destiny in the form of a roulette wheel, with the clarity of a revelation. From a man with no depth, he becomes one who seems to comprehend everything in Malraux's philosophy, in one experience.

> He had the feeling of seizing his life, of holding it suspended to the whim of that absurd ball . . . the living reality . . . of every-thing by which men believe their destinies to be governed. . . . Through its agency he was embracing his own destiny—the only means he had ever found of possessing himself!

Yet a sense of wrongness, of a false twist in his revelation, seeps through to us: he is gratifying "at once the two Clappiques that composed him, the one who wanted to live and the one who wanted to be destroyed"; he tries to win "no longer in order to take flight, but to remain, to risk more, so that the stake of his conquered liberty would render the gesture even more absurd!" He finds in gambling "a suicide without death." Knowing that his play will lead to his own inability to leave Shanghai and to Kyo's capture,

> he threw Kyo back into a world of dreams . . . he was sustaining that ball . . . with his own life . . . and with the life of another. . . . He knew he was sacrificing Kyo; it was Kyo who was chained to that ball, to that table, and it was he, Clappique, who was that ball, which was master of everyone and of himself— of himself who was nevertheless looking at it, living as he had never lived, outside of himself, held spellbound and breathless by an overpowering shame.

His liberation begins to seem false to him the moment he leaves the gam-bling house; "anguish was returning"; he tries to defend himself by going from prostitute to prostitute, concocting a tale of his own coming suicide, becoming drunk on his fabrications of "a world where truth no longer existed . . . neither true nor false, but real." Again his old metaphysics argues that since this new universe did not exist, "nothing existed. The world had ceased to weigh upon him. Liberated, he lived now only in the romantic universe which he had just created."

Much later he returns to his room, trying to banish torment and solitude with whiskey. He spies a mirror and, in a weirdly terrifying scene, "as if he had found a way of expressing directly in all its intensity the torment which words were not adequate to translate, he began to make faces transforming himself . . . into all the grotesques that a human face can express," then suddenly recoils from the "frightful mirror" whose "debauchery of the grotesque . . . was assuming the atrocious and terrifying humor of madness."

He feels no remorse, only a fear of death; having lost his money, he destroys his identity by passing himself off as a sailor on a vessel about to depart, preferring, as a stowaway, a voyage that will probably lead to prison to his real physical annihilation; and aboard ship he returns to his continuing round of mythomania and alcohol. He stands firm on his conviction that "men do not exist" because "a costume is enough to enable one to escape from oneself"—even though that escape is only the construction and reconstruction of a series of prisons. Clappique might have been able to alter his life, to emerge from his self-imposed regime of degradation, if he had cared to notice the chance and to will the change. Instead, and despite a series of insights into the sources of his anguish, he has chosen—and knows he would choose again—one more, and the grandest, of a series of abject illusions of liberation, "the most dazzling success of his life," since he is no longer telling a lie but existing as one. He is a figure out of surrealist quietism, and his nonviolent confrontation with destiny, his absurd reaction to absurdity, is a form of subjection and submission that scarcely pretends to be anything else.

Another character who follows an escapist road away from his own overwhelming angst is Kyo's father, Old Gisors. An intellectual, he has organized revolutionary cadres but avoids action himself. Quite unlike his son (or Garine), he is a contemplative, interested in what is deepest or most singular in men rather than in what can be used to make them act, in individual men rather than in the moving forces of the world of flux. His meeting with other major characters—Clappique, Ch'en, Kyo, Ferral—all turn into analyses which the reader may accept as true but which lead to no conclusions. And these disjoined analyses are but one step away from a total lack of contact; it is only his son who binds him to the world of men and makes them matter at all, and after Kyo's death human individuals no longer exist for him at all.

At the outset Old Gisors is a Marxist for reasons precisely opposed to those of Kyo, for a fear of death brings to him a consciousness of fatality; rather than revolt against this fatality, he wishes to bring himself into harmony with it; while Kyo lives and men still count for something to him, Gisors is therefore attracted to Marxism, not by the will it contains, but by its element of fatality. As for the men he scrutinizes, however much he knows or deduces about them, he does not know them. He begins with the abstract cognition of the distance lying between himself and others. As the revolution begins, he comes to apply this realization, to feel the gap, to understand that he does not know his own son, that there is no point of contact between them even though they are on the same side of a political contest. As a former professor, he can be sure only of what he has taught or given to a man, and it is not he who has taught Kyo to follow the life of action. He loves his son ("One never knows a human being, but one occasionally ceases to feel that one does not know him"), he teaches his students to give themselves wholly to the *willing* side of Marxism, solely to give Kyo allies; but his love cannot overcome the separation he perceives between them, his own consequent solitude, anguish, and obsession with death.

A photograph of Kyo lies under the tray which holds Gisors's real escape: opium. Since he cannot escape his total solitude, since he can neither reach nor be reached by another consciousness, he chooses to plumb the depths of his own "furious subterranean imagination" clothed in the benign indifference of the drug. The oppressive world loses its bitterness to his perceptions: "His eyes shut, carried by great motionless wings, Gisors contemplated his solitude: a desolation that joined the divine, while at the same time the wave of serenity that gently covered the depths of death widened to infinity." When Kyo is captured, Gisors makes hopeless attempts to secure his release; after Kyo's death he is plunged into grief but refuses at first to smother it with opium. He watches near his son's body and allows the meaninglessness of the world to burn out and destroy all the bonds which had linked it to him; "he felt the basic suffering trembling within him, not that which comes from creatures or from things, but that which gushes forth from man himself and from which life attempts to tear us away."

But at the last he flees to Japan and to opium again; he abandons his Marxism and becomes indifferent finally to life and death. " 'Men should be able to learn that there is no reality, that there are worlds of contemplation—with or without opium—where all is vain!' 'Where one contemplates what?' 'Perhaps nothing other than this vanity. . . . That's a great deal.' . . . 'All suffer, and each one suffers because he thinks. At bottom, the mind conceives man only in the eternal, and the consciousness of life can be nothing but anguish. One must not think of life with the mind, but with opium.' " He becomes able to view Kyo's death without torture. " 'It takes fifty years to make a man, fifty years of sacrifice, of will. . . . And when this man is complete, when there is nothing left in him of childhood . . . when he is really a man . . . he is good for nothing but to die.' " He contemplates men whom he no longer resembles and achieves an understanding from his distance of

> all those unknown creatures who were marching toward death in the dazzling sunlight, each one nursing his deadly parasite in a secret recess of his being. "Every man is a madman . . . but what is human destiny if not a life of effort to unite this madman and the universe. . . . Every man dreams of being god." . . . Humanity was dense and heavy, heavy with flesh, with blood, with suffering, eternally clinging to itself like all that dies, but even blood, even flesh, even suffering, even death was being absorbed up there in the light like music in the silent night . . . human grief seemed to him to rise and to lose itself in the very song of earth; upon the quivering release hidden within him like his heart, the grief which he had mastered—slowly closed its inhuman arms.

He sees men, but he has lost them; his escape has cut him off from all that is human in them: "for the first time the idea that the time which was bringing him closer to death was flowing through him did not isolate him from the world, but joined him to it in a serene accord. . . . Liberated from everything, even from being a man, he caressed the stem of his pipe." Like his son's dead body, he is "already something other than a man."

Clappique and Old Gisors seek to escape by transforming their awareness of the world. Clappique's weapons are alcohol and lies, Gisors's are drugs. Clappique concocts fabulous tales about himself to deny life, to support his principle that "nothing exists: all is dream." He drinks to create a dream, he gambles to achieve the sense of victory and liberation. By mythomania and alcohol he constructs a series of spurious illusions of freedom—a series of degradations and submissions and self-imposed humiliations, lies which at last he can neither believe nor escape. Gisors, like Clappique, resolves the struggle between man and the world, between self and otherness, by merging man with world, self with otherness. Like Clappique, he escapes by a voluntary destruction of himself, akin to suicide: he is finished with the struggle and pain of being a man. Men must strive and suffer always, if not the one then the other; those who leave off doing either become foreign to mankind. And whether the escape is effected by self-brutalization or self-transcendence makes no difference, for a completely successful escape, like a death, closes the books on a human existence.

Power, violence, lies, and dreams do not escape the judgment of destiny. The third group of characters, the true revolutionaries, even in the face of their own humiliations and deaths grasp human and permanent values. Malraux, with a new "social" consciousness, discovers a human type for whom human isolation is neither necessary nor eternal: in the present it can be broken in a common struggle, even in a common defeat; in the future, toward which that struggle is directed, it may be withered by the transformation of civilization.

In his life Kyo Gisors fights for a value that will outlive him—the "human dignity" that is the just common property of all man. He conceives of dignity primarily as a negation, the absence of the humiliation of man by man, the end of the absurd cycle of being humiliated and of humiliating, of being tortured and torturing, that describes the life of König or of Ferral, or of Garine. The implication of a struggle for "human dignity" instead of for "my dignity" (which for König lies in "humiliating them") is a utopian anarchism, an opposition, not to government, but to the urge of the powerful to compel. Garine knows of only one way not to be beaten—to conquer. Kyo subscribes to a third path. He does not elaborate on the changes that would have to be made in the social order or in the psyches of individuals of the conquering and escapist types before the utopia of dignity could come to be. But he cannot take the problem of the future as seriously as he might because physical victory in the present is not achieved in the novel. Therefore the utopia of human dignity remains at the level of a Sorelian myth, emphasizing and driving a will to act in the present rather than describing in detail the future brought by victorious action.

Yet the hopeful future is not left so vague as this. Malraux himself reveals a subdued utopianism, introducing hope, not only through Kyo, but also through Old Gisors and Hemmelrich. In one of his detached analyses Gisors declares that a civilization becomes transformed when its most oppressed element suddenly becomes a *value* and that for modern civilization this will occur when the worker ceases to attempt to escape his work and finds in it his reason for being—when the factory becomes what the cathedral was, and men see in it, not gods, but human power struggling against the earth. And Hemmelrich, driven into Russia after the suppression of the Shanghai uprising, fulfills Old Gisors's prophetic words by discovering his own dignity in the work that had previously crushed him—because for the

first time "I work and know why I work." The inference is that the transformed future will involve not merely sociopolitical transformations of an
anarchist sort (the abolition of the institutionalized opportunity to dominate)
and psychological changes (the healing of the Conquerors), but new cultural
myths as well.

Myths appear in many forms in Malraux's work. Myths about the
heroic life of an individual inspire initiates to imitate him; such myths, thus
far, have only appeared as damaging, since they have attached themselves
only to Conquerors (as in the Grabot-Perken-Claude chain). Myths about
a new future and a good life therein have been manipulated by psycho-
technicians to procure them power (Garine). Such myths, of a future in
which the content of the good life is absolute personal power, accepted by
the Conquerors, have stirred them to action and struggle but have always
yielded defeat, though at moments the presence of the other men whom
he is using in the fight has broken through to the Conqueror and has revealed
to him some real value, which he normally passes by. Myths about men
and the world dominate whole cultures: the Western myth leads to anguish
and despair for those who believe it (according to Ling) and for those who
do not. But Malraux, perhaps because of his early anthropological training,
cannot espouse the impossible—a civilization without myths. Instead he
has begun the search for new, potentially creative myths, at all three levels:
hero myths, political-utopia myths, and cultural myths. The first possible
hero myth (the Conqueror-type) has been tried and found wanting; Malraux
is now examining the second type. He has only just begun a reflection on
a political utopia of dignity: one feature of that utopia will be a cultural
myth that destroys the alienation of the worker from his work by explaining
it, not as something he must do to keep alive and get cash, but as a role in
a common struggle. Since this is a peaceable utopia, the worker is to be
animated not by a class-struggle myth (as with Sorel and Stalinism) nor by
one of national struggle, but by a myth of the struggle of man against the
earth—a humanist myth. Gisors's lecture on the transformation of a civilization is the first sign of what is to become Malraux's humanist position,
in which the Western cultural myth described by Ling ("men" as separate
from and in conflict with "the world," and the "individual" as separate
from and in conflict with all other "individuals") is to be supplanted by a
myth of "man" as a naturally harmonious unity separate from, and as a
whole in conflict with, "the world."

But, because the political order of the moment offers no immediate
chance to bring about the better world, the mythic heroes of Man's Fate
do not conduct a revolution to victory and build a new order: they follow

it to defeat and find a new value. The political utopia they seek is not within sight: but, in making them struggle for a good future, it yields them part of its values in the present. This situation is partly exemplified by Hemmelrich and by the Russian Organization Man, Katov, and fully by the death of the Franco-Japanese intellectual, Kyo Gisors.

The shopkeeper and phonograph seller Hemmelrich is an ambiguous character: almost the counterpart of König, through half-ironic and uncontrollable, half-unexplained means he has managed to hold back and win over the dehumanizing forces around him. For thirty-seven years he has lived unable to rise above wretchedness, "a blind and persecuted dog." If he could, he would "offset by violence—any kind of violence . . . this atrocious life that has poisoned him since he was born, that would poison his children in the same way." But he cannot join the revolution and die, because of his wife—whom he married because she was as wretched as he—and their child, sick with mastoiditis and in constant pain. He cannot strike back; out of fear for them he cannot even give shelter to his friends.

> If he had had money, if he could have left it to them, he would have been free to go and get killed. As if the universe had not treated him all his life with kicks in the belly, it now despoiled him of the only dignity he could ever possess—his death.

But when the repression begins, his shop is "cleaned out" by grenades in his absence, his wife and child are killed; an ironic fate has freed him. "He could not banish from his mind the atrocious, weighty, profound joy of liberation . . . now he was no longer impotent. Now, *he too could kill.*" He runs to the nearest Communist strongpoint to help in its defense. There is an explosion; he recovers consciousness to see a Blue scout coming toward him through the barbed wire, an opportunity to kill. "He was no longer a man, he was everything that Hemmelrich had suffered from until now. . . . 'They have made us starve all our lives, but this one is going to get it, he's going to get it. . . . You'll pay for it!' " He kills the man and escapes in his uniform.

Hemmelrich might now be ready to join König as a man capable of nothing but killing; yet, inexplicably, this one murder appears to bring his second, and real, liberation. His hands, covered with the blood of his family, had been horrors which could only be forgotten if he held a knife or a machine gun in them; but now two drops of blood from the man he has killed fall in turn on the victim's hands, "and as if this hand that was being spattered with blood had avenged him, Hemmelrich dared at last to look at his own, and discovered that the blood-stain had rubbed off hours before." Unlike König, Hemmelrich is able to stop at this juncture without making himself once more a subject of the Absurd. He leaves China, and the reader is told that he has finally found what becomes in this novel Malraux's foremost value—his dignity—in work.

> "He is a mounter in the electric plant. He said to me: 'Before, I began to live when I left the factory; now, I begin to live when I enter it. It's the first time in my life that I work and know why I work, not merely waiting patiently to die.' "

Hemmelrich has been freed; more importantly, he has been able to free himself.

Malraux's Organization Men (Comintern professional revolutionaries) have tended to be moral mediocrities who are skillful at explaining why revolutionaries must compromise to survive and why foreign revolutions must be subordinated to the welfare of the Soviet Union. But Katov (and Kassner of *Days of Wrath*) transcend mediocrity through suffering. By the time of the Spanish Civil War all the old questions and more arise: but in these two novels the Organization Men are permitted to surpass themselves.

Katov, unlike the other Shanghai insurrectionists, has already been freed of his burden of anguish. This burden, like that of Hemmelrich, was the suffering of others whom he could not relieve; as Hemmelrich is freed in the course of the novel, Katov had long since been liberated by death to fight. He knows what he is fighting for: every battle now recalls to him a memory from the Russian Civil War—the capture of his battalion in winter, the digging of their own graves, their taking off coats and trousers in the cold before the White firing squad, the uncontrollable sneezes "so intensely human, in that dawn of execution, that the machine-gunners waited— waited for life to become less indiscreet." The other Organization Men act in the name of a fatality, the inevitable Revolution; Katov acts in the name and memory of men. With his fellows, Katov is captured in the repression. Almost nothing is known about him when he finally appears in a school-yard, used to hold the wounded prisoners waiting to be shot, and is put with Kyo in a space reserved for those who are to be tortured to death by being thrown alive into the boiler of a locomotive—their deaths signaled back to those in the schoolyard by the shriek of the locomotive whistle. It is the way of his living those last hours which says all there is to be said about him. "Katov was lying . . . beside him, separated from him by the vast expanse of suffering" which separates all, but also "joined to him by that absolute friendship, without reticence, which death alone gives . . . among all those brothers in the mendicant order of the Revolution: each of these men had wildly seized as it stalked past him the only greatness that could be his." When Kyo dies beside him, Katov is thrown back into solitude, but without suffering. He too has cyanide with which to end his life; but next to him are two of his fellows without it, and in the grip of fear.

> In spite of all these men who had fought as he had, Katov was alone, alone between the body of his dead friend and his two terror-stricken companions, alone between this wall and the whistle far off in the night. But a man could be stronger than this solitude and even, perhaps, than that atrocious whistle: fear struggled in him against the most terrible temptation in his life.

He gives them the cyanide and condemns himself. Katov is a doctrinaire among the revolutionaries, but nothing in his doctrine obliged him to make that sacrifice, and it puts him on a plane above both those who decline to act and those whose action relates to themselves alone.

His Japanese education gave Kyo Gisors the conviction that "ideas were not to be thought, but lived." He has taken up his manner of living through a conscious and voluntary act rather than under a compulsion (like Ch'en). "Kyo had chosen action, in a grave and premeditated way, as others choose a military career, or the sea: he left his father, lived in Canton, in Tientsin, the life of day-laborers and coolies, in order to organize the syndicates." He is a different type from the nihilist-adventurers and terrorists. He is not restless; since he is not secretly in love with death, he does not use the idea of a heroic life to justify continuing to live; the heroic sense merely gives him a form of discipline in action. The Absurd is not his constant companion: "His life had a meaning, and he knew what it was: to give to each of those men whom famine, at this very moment, was killing off like a slow plague, a sense of his own dignity." Thus he rejects the most debilitating element of Western cultural consciousness and affirms its most humanistic potential values. The oppression that was grist for the propaganda mill of Garine—who only half understood the value he was communicating to the Chinese masses—becomes for Kyo the real enemy, and Old Gisors's utopian hope in a sense becomes a destination. " 'There is no possible dignity, no real life for a man who works twelve hours a day without knowing why he works.' That work would have to take on a meaning, become a faith." Katov coordinates the insurrection along with Kyo; but Kyo has more of a sense of its possible meaning: the revolt is intended "to conquer here the dignity of his people."

The author shows more of Kyo, who is the deeper character, and therefore the reader becomes aware that this new type of hero is not someone who has had a fortuitous escape from his humanity. He too can be tormented: a phonograph becomes the symbol of his transient obsession. Having made a recording of his own voice, he finds that he cannot recognize it when it is played back to him. The occurrence nags at the depth of his consciousness, and he questions his father about it. " 'It's undoubtedly a question of means: we hear the voices of others with our ears.' 'And our own?' 'With our throats: for you can hear your own voice with your ears stopped.' " And then: " 'Opium is also a world we do not hear with our ears.' " And later the event comes back to him in a moment of self-doubt:

> His torment returned, and he remembered the records: "We hear the voices of others with our ears, our own voices with our throats." Yes. One hears his own life, too, with his throat, and those of others? . . . First of all there was solitude, the inescapable aloneness behind the living multitude. . . . "But I, to my throat, what am I? A kind of absolute, the affirmation of an idiot: an intensity greater than all the rest. To others, I am what I have done."

But there is a reason for this torment, and it passes when Kyo is able to overcome its real cause.

Kyo—the first of Malraux's heroes able to feel toward a woman more than an eroticism which is really a relation of himself to himself—is deeply in love with his wife, May. She is, like him, a revolutionary (and it is not by chance that the ability to love is combined with a commitment to revolution). "For more than a year May had freed him from all solitude, if not from all bitterness." His brief convulsion of despair and futility is brought on when she tells him on the morning of the insurrection that in the face of suffering and death she has just gone to bed with another man. He is consumed, not by real jealousy or hatred (since he understands her only too well), but by a feeling of being suddenly separated from her, of being unable to find her: she has returned him to solitude.

In his tormented meditation Kyo stumbles on a suggestive psychology of love: it is to May only that he exists as something more than a biographical summary of his actions; in the same way that Old Gisors is able to know in others what he has changed in them and made of them, Kyo and May are able to know each other because they love each other, and this ability has been their mutual defense against solitude.

> "My kind are those who love me and do not look at me, who love me in spite of everything, degradation, baseness, treason—

me and not what I have done or shall do—who would love me as long as I love myself—even to suicide. . . . With her alone I have this love in common. . . ." It was not happiness, certainly. It was something primitive which was at one with the darkness and caused a warmth to rise in him, resolving itself into a motionless embrace . . . the only thing in him that was as strong as death.

Not until the collapse of the revolt, when Kyo goes out to be captured, does he regain this relation with May: he refuses to allow her to accompany him, under the guise of protecting her; there is a moment of total separation, until she motions to him to go; finding that his torment only recurs, he returns for her, having learned "that the willingness to lead the being one loves to death itself is perhaps the complete expression of love, that which cannot be surpassed." Because this love is sufficient for him, before he dies—alone—he regrets only that May, who is weaker than he, must be left alone with her grief. That Kyo is able to build, and to rebuild, such a relation is enough to show his difference from those who can only suffer or "triumph" alone.

As with Katov, more is revealed about Kyo when the apparent victory of the insurrection is transformed into defeat, and he determines to die for it, than before. He is captured and faced first with humiliation—the same sort of humiliation which has brutalized his interrogator König—and then with death. The humiliation comes when he is thrown into a temporary prison: darkness, the odor of a slaughterhouse, wooden cages, and within them "men, like worms," and the warder with his whip. Because all the prisoners are utterly powerless before him, the warder takes on the shape of a bestial incarnation of fatality. Kyo witnesses the flogging of an old harmless lunatic, is helpless to prevent it, and horribly and ignominiously must struggle against a desire to watch the torture. But he is able to stop the beating, then to endure his own whipping and then to have his slashed hand shaken by the torturer. "Life had never imposed upon him anything more hideous"; yet, simply by departing from the prison, he is able to leave behind that "loathsome part of himself" which has been created there. After this, it is not merely a pompous gesture when he tells König:

> "I think that Communism will make dignity possible for those with whom I am fighting. What is against it, at any rate, forces them to have none. . . ." "What do you call dignity? It doesn't mean anything." . . . "The opposite of humiliation. . . . When one comes from where I come, that means something."

Like Katov, like Hemmelrich after the death of his wife and child, Kyo Gisors is a free man. He is aware of the presence of the Absurd, but he is not obsessed by it, he is not a compulsive killer or liar or addict or master. When he does feel anguish, it is for a specific reason, not because he is an unhappy consciousness, and if the reason passes, so does anguish. At the last he knows that dying in the common fight for dignity can be an act as exalted as any act in life and that there would have been no value in his life had he not been ready to die for it.

> He had fought for what was in his time charged with the deepest meaning and the greatest hope; he was dying among those with whom he would have wanted to live; he was dying, like each of these men, because he had given a meaning to his life. . . . It is easy to die when one does not die alone. A death saturated with this brotherly quavering, an assembly of the vanquished in which multitudes will recognize their martyrs, a bloody legend of which the golden legends are made!

Kyo has made a success of his life. He cannot avoid, as no man can avoid, the final fatality, but even that he seizes, rather than accepting as it is thrust on him. His life, which could have been made meaningless if he had let fatality or events, oppression or despair or discipline, make it so, has a meaning because he has made a meaning for it. He exists in solitude because he is an individual, but he overcomes that solitude in the company of those who had shared first victory and then defeat and who, prisoners, are now to share death. One bond links them in spite of all the movements of events that tend to separate or degrade them: "fraternity," the immediate communion among human persons converted into a fellowship by direct confrontation with a common fate. Kyo's life is an image to others because he has not merely had a hope, as Gisors had, but has fought for its realization, and because its realization would involve a value above self-concern and self-love and even self-fulfillment. He has struggled to procure for others a dignity which is native to him; his death is as worthy of him as is his life; he is, in short, a political hero of the highest type shown in Malraux's works.

That type may be called the Bolshevik hero. His solitude is a contingent condition, with which he breaks by action. If his action is successful, it may lead to a new social order in which isolation and malaise will be contingent and conquerable for all men. Because his action is directed to that end, his will has given a meaning to his life; because his life has a meaning, he is not perpetually restless. Because he fights in common for a common hope, he can even in physical defeat breach solitude and attain fraternity, the present good that is his reward for seeking the future good. From the display of human types and ways of life a high myth, a political commitment, has emerged.

The mythic Bolshevik hero collects and reconciles fragments from Malraux's past. He captures the fraternity that Claude felt by chance and the meaning in life and death that Perken grasped for one single moment. He creates men's souls as Garine did, but he possesses the hope that Garine manipulated. He holds the values that the Conquerors overlooked. One may wonder about some of his more obscure features. Can he remain a Communist when the party is run by the Organization Men? What will really happen to a society where the Bolsheviks are victorious? On such a day, what will become of the fraternity of the elite revolutionary intellectuals? The workers will find meaningful work: what will the dignity of the few consist in, once the persecutors whose repressions aroused their fraternal sentiments are gone? But in Malraux's next novel such questions are not relevant because victory is still not in sight. His second hero-type thus attains a temporary stability, and his political thought finds a first resting place.

Days of Wrath (1935) returns to the single-main-character pattern, this time with a positive figure at the center. The work deals with nine days spent by a German Communist, Kassner, in a Nazi prison cell. *Days of Wrath* is a natural successor to *Man's Fate;* it contains none of the ideological conflict of the earlier work, but it contains the resolution of that conflict. Kassner, like Katov, is a man committed without the constancy of anguished doubt that has rightly accompanied the commitments of others. Because he is not so deep a man as Kyo, his book is a lesser one; but he adds more substance to the figure of the Bolshevik hero.

The intellectual structure of *Days of Wrath* is unlike that of the previous single-hero books. Instead of an anguished vision, a revolt, and a defeat, there is a revolt, a sacrifice, an escape, and a new revolt. Kassner is an organizer of the German Communist underground. He is arrested when he deliberately springs a police trap to save his comrades. He is imprisoned, questioned, tortured, and isolated. If the insane fantasies born of his solitude do not kill him, the Nazis will. But an unknown comrade saves him from madness by establishing communication with him through the cell walls; another saves his life by assuming his identity and his place in prison. Outside Germany Kassner is reunited with his wife at a mass meeting of his comrades, and he prepares to return to Germany.

At one level this book is a work of propaganda: the brotherhood of mutual sacrifice in which the Communists are united preserves them from the impacts of life and death, permits them to overcome the fear of death, to overcome torture and solitude. The party (whether or not it ever existed on earth) makes its men into brothers and heroes. At this level *Days of Wrath* is a skillful lyric peroration to the dramatics of *Man's Fate*. The only question of special interest is why Kassner is an Organization Man, why the movement proceeds from Kyo, who rejects the dead weight of the apparatus of the International, to Kassner, a man wholly within the organization, with no sense of conflict between its objectives and his own, no qualms about his position.

Malraux's heroes, like Malraux himself, seek a good in political action which they cannot secure by their own power. Repeatedly they must choose as allies political forces stronger than themselves. The force chosen is that which comes closest to providing the desired goal; the intimacy of the alliance depends upon the similarity of the goals of individual and movement. Garine wanted to overthrow an old order of power and take it for himself. He allied himself with the Kuomintang Communists because they were both passionate and competent: but after a joint success he and they would have become rivals. By 1927 and the Shanghai affair the Comintern had lost its passion, but the revolutionaries on the spot had not. And Kyo wants something different—"human dignity": he believes that the Communists may supply it while their enemies will certainly not. In 1934–35 the Comintern had a short-lived "humanist" outburst which suggested that its explicit positive goal might not be far from Malraux's (it was at this time that he was honored in Moscow); that trend was followed by the policy of the popular front, which recaptured for the Communists in the eyes of many the "will" and activism they had lost at the time of *Man's Fate*. On the basis of the behavior and misbehavior of the Communist apparatus alone, therefore, it was valid to portray Kassner as a Communist, because at this time there existed no other political force which could or would do what Malraux wanted done. It was on the same ground that in 1948 Malraux defended his alignment with De Gaulle. In 1935 it was the Communists who, in carrying on the struggle for a valid future, permitted even such ordinary men as Kassner to live heroic lives and to enjoy the fraternity of heroes. To convey that fact is one intention of *Days of Wrath*.

But at a level less bound to current events there is a more universal intent, which can outlast the conditions of a current alliance. (Like the elements of the first two novels that are preserved and developed, this aspect is present in fragmentary form.) At this universal level the matter of chance that Kassner is at a certain moment a Communist is unimportant. In the preface Malraux speaks of "the world of tragedy, the ancient world," composed of man, what oppresses him (the elements, isolation, destiny, death) and what defends him. Kassner is simply fundamental man: his successive trials are meant to be typical of the ordeal of men before the everyday risk of death, and his defenses—comradeship, fraternity, love— are meant to be recourses universally and eternally valid. Kassner is a worker by social origin, an intellectual only by self-education—Malraux's first such hero. Even the most oppressed of men in the most oppressive of states can have what is needful to combat his suffering; even he can choose the right life and death.

When doubts return about the virtues of the apparat, the almost serene acceptance of a conclusion to political debate will not persist. *Man's Hope* explodes the passing resolution of all political problems expressed in *Days of Wrath*. But Kassner was able to transcend his isolation outside as well as inside the frame of politics. He feels a sense of communion, not only with his fellow sufferers, but also with the woman he loves, with a crowd, with a pilot in a storm. Politics is not essential to personal "salvation" in every case: for the Absurd has many faces, as Garine knew very well. The revolutionaries in *Man's Fate* have almost forgotten this truth, for each of them is the victim of one chief form of absurdity, its political form. Kassner sees many forms again: in the face of oppression and torture, of the inhuman power of nature, of the madness of the crowds, of the certainty of death, he is able to work an inner change by reflection, to conceive in each case a different communion and a different defense. Where there are brothers, therefore, it will be possible for men to transcend their isolation by political action so long as they are subjected to a common and indiscriminate oppression; but it does not necessarily follow that where oppression is not felt in common or where isolation is not political, isolation and oppression cannot be transcended. Communion comes through politics in *Man's Fate*. Some other areas of life afford it in *Days of Wrath,* though only peripherally.

The moments of self-transcendence afforded to the insurrectionists of *Man's Fate* turn into a lifetime of such moments in the permanent underground of *Days of Wrath.* So long as a vigorous, united, and consciously repressive state machine confronts, persecutes, but cannot destroy an organized resistance, these rebels and brothers can be compelled to lead short, happy lives as individuals and a long, lyrical existence as a group. Because victory is not in sight, they need not trouble themselves with difficult political questions. Because circumstances permit them to identify a certain ruling class as oppressors, and a certain oppressed class as brothers, they have only to act, only to keep the faith, and they are healed. Their health depends on the existence of a cruel, deliberately oppressive, but inefficient regime (for so the Nazis are presented). If the revolutionaries were to win, they must needs take thought, as becomes clear in Malraux's next novel. But what if the Kassners (and the Kyos and the Katovs) had no such oppressive order, no such clear-cut enemies and comrades? Such was the situation of Garine: he traveled to find a revolution, but it was not his; he attained no lasting communion. And what if there is no "clearly" just cause, no self-evident and self-conscious community of the oppressed, no painstaking and deliberate persecution?

When the historical circumstances require it, Malraux turns to answer these questions. New means of transcending the human situation will continue to reveal themselves, far more fully than they do to Kassner. So long as a delicate balance of social forces permits it, the Bolshevik remains a hero. Either victory or tolerance would derange that balance. When they do, the Bolshevik becomes an incomplete hero, and another replaces him— a more rounded and varied human type.

The Structure
of *La Condition humaine*

Lucien Goldmann

Appearing after *Les Conquérants* and *La Voie royale,* this third novel [*La Condition humaine*] was to have an enormous impact and made Malraux famous throughout the world.

Although it is still what I have called one of the "transitional" novels (between the novel with a problematic hero and the novel without character), and although the subject is still, as in *Les Conquérants,* the Chinese revolution, the world of *La Condition humaine* is, in relation to the two preceding novels, entirely different.

Was the author influenced by his discussion with Trotsky? It is, of course, impossible to establish this with any certainty. Nevertheless, the work is in certain respects—but *only in certain respects*—fairly close to the Trotskyist point of view.

But however important an element the "chronicle of the revolution" is (and it is much more important in *La Condition humaine* than in *Les Conquérants*), it remains, in the final resort, of secondary importance for a structuralist or even a merely literary analysis. The true novelty of the book lies in the fact that, in relation to the worlds of *La Voie royale* and *Les Conquérants,* which were governed by the problem of the hero's individual realization, the world of *La Condition humaine* is governed by quite other laws and above all by a different value: *that of the revolutionary community*.

Let us approach the essential point at once: as a novel in the strictest sense of the word, *La Condition humaine* has a problematic hero, but, as a novel of transition, it describes for us, not an individual but a *collective problematic character:* the community of Shanghai revolutionaries represented in the narrative primarily by three individual characters, Kyo, Katow, and May, but also Hemmelrich and by all the anonymous militants by whom we know they are surrounded.

A *collective* and *problematic* hero; this characteristic, which makes *La Condition humaine* a true novel, derives from the fact that the Shanghai revolutionaries are attached to the essential and, in the world of the novel, contradictory requirements: on the one hand, the deepening and development of the revolution and, on the other hand, discipline towards the Party and the International.

But the Party and the International are engaged in a purely defensive policy. They are strictly opposed to any revolutionary action in the city, withdraw the troops that are faithful to them, and demand the handing back of arms to Chiang Kai-shek, although, quite plainly, Chiang is planning to assassinate the Communist leaders and militants.

In these conditions, it is inevitable that the Shanghai militants should turn to defeat and massacre.

In so far as the book is *also* a "chronicle of the revolution," one sees why its point of view is *fairly close* to the thinking of the Communist opposition. It is written from the point of view of Kyo, May, Katow, and their comrades and implicitly stresses the sabotage of their struggle by the leadership of the Party and the responsibility of this leadership for the defeat, massacre, and torture of the militants.

In this framework, the value that governs the world of *La Condition humaine* is that of the *community,* which is, of course, the *community of the revolutionary struggle.*

Since the world in which the action unfolds is the same as that of *Les Conquérants,* the characters—with a few minor exceptions—are necessarily the same, though they are seen from a quite different point of view. So, in order to illuminate them more clearly, it might be useful to analyse them in turn, situating each of them in relation to the corresponding character of the preceding novel.

We will begin, of course, with the main character: the group of revolutionaries. In *Les Conquérants,* it was personified by Borodin. The difference is obvious enough, but it is justified by the difference of perspective.

As seen by the individualist Garine, the revolutionary can only be *an individual* whose distinctive feature is the fact that he is not only closely linked to the proletariat and to the organization that directs the revolution, but also that he goes so far as to identify himself with this proletariat and this revolution, whereas, *seen from the inside,* this distinctive feature is specifically what transforms the individual into a community. So the story related in *La Condition humaine* is not only that of the action carried out by Kyo, May, Katow, and their comrades, the history of their defeat and death, but also, closely bound up with this action, the history of their community, which is a living dynamic psychical reality.

Around them, if we leave to one side certain incidental figures, we will meet four characters who belong to no community and who remain more or less isolated individuals: an ally, the Chinese terrorist Chen, an enemy, Ferral, and two intermediary characters, Clappique and Gisors.

I have just written "an *ally,* the Chinese terrorist Chen," whereas in *Les Conquérants,* Hong remained in spite of everything an *enemy* whom Garine—in spite of all his sympathy—was finally to execute. The difference derives from the fact that, far from being Hong's homologue, Chen is a mixture of Hong and Garine, a mixture in which the elements related to those that made up the personality of Garine are predominant. This is explained and, indeed, justified by the same difference of perspective. Seen with Garine's eyes, the difference between him and Hong was considerable. Hong, in effect, has an abstract attitude, alien to any concern for efficacity, whereas Garine could find meaning—however precarious and provisional—in his existence only in revolutionary action entirely subordinated to the *efficacity* of the struggle.

From Borodin's point of view, however, this difference loses much of its importance. Hong and Garine resemble one another in so far as they are both individuals who, though declared and active enemies of the bougeoisie, nevertheless do not identify themselves with the revolution.

On the side of the enemies of the revolution, only one character is really present in the novel: Ferral, who directs an industrial consortium, helps to overthrow Chiang Kai-shek's alliances and organizes the agreement between Chiang and the Shanghai bourgeoisie. He is a character of the *conqueror* type but, of course, a much more superficial conqueror than Garine and Perkin, since instead of rallying to the revolution he has committed himself to the side of false values, to what, in the novel, embodies evil and lies. In fact, he really represents one of the risks to which this human type is exposed, a risk that had been touched on in *Les Conquérants* by Nikolaieff when he suggested to the narrator that Garine might have become a "Mussolinian."

Lastly, between the revolutionaries and reaction, two characters in the novel occupy a fairly important position: Gisors, Kyo's father, and Clappique. Clappique is an old acquaintance who had disappeared from Malraux's two preceding novels. He personifies the aerostats and deadly sins of *Lunes en Papier,* the man who lived in imagination; the nonconformist artist, the buffoon. It should be said, however, that at the time he was writing *La Condition humaine,* Malraux had much more sympathy for him than at the period of *Lunes en Papier.* This, too, can be explained: *Lunes en Papier* is an attempt to unmask people who claimed to be only valid revolutionaries in a world in which there was no place for hope, whereas now Clappique, between the revolutionaries on the one hand, and Chiang Kai-shek or Ferral on the other, acts more or less as a sort of gadfly. Nevertheless, we must admire a writer who, despite his sympathy for Clappique, is quite merciless in showing that his attitude of detachment from reality, while useful at times, may also be detrimental, even fatal, to the revolutionaries fighting for authentic values.

Gisors embodies the old Chinese culture, which is, in the last resort, alien to all violence, whether reactionary or revolutionary. In relation to *Les Conquérants,* he really corresponds to Chen-Dai. But he is a very real character and this correspondence is more complex and more mediatized than in the case of the other characters. Chen-Dai was opposed on principle to revolutionary violence. Gisors, on the contrary, is bound to the revolution not directly—for ideological reasons—but out of affection for his son who is committed to it body and soul. Now it seems to me that we have here two *complementary* aspects of old China and it would be impossible to imagine Gisors in *Les Conquérants* or Chen-Dai in *La Condition humaine.* Nevertheless, there is a structural reason in favour of the solution adopted by Malraux: *Les Conquérants* describes the victory of the revolution, *La Condition humaine* its defeat. Now it is of the essence of the Gisors and Chen-Dais of this world to be opposed to victorious violence and to find themselves, rather ineffectively no doubt, on the side of the defeated.

The plot of the novel, although poignant and tragic, is simple enough: faced with the advance of the Kuomintang army (which *still* comprises both Chiang Kai-shek and the Chinese Communist Party) the clandestine organization of the Shanghai Communists, supported by the trade unions, is planning an uprising intended both to facilitate the victory of the attackers and, at the same time, to get control of the leadership of the movement *after* victory. In fact, the conflict between Chiang Kai-shek and the Communists became increasingly sharp as the victory of the Kuomintang became imminent. Having been united in a struggle between a common enemy, they will now have to solve the problem of the social and political structures of the new China that the defeat of its enemy will leave as the major problem.

An important section of the militants of the Chinese Party, and among them, the Shanghai revolutionaries, organized the peasants and unions by promising to the first agrarian reforms and to the second the seizure of power in the towns. In order to resist them and to maintain control of the Kuomintang, Chiang Kai-shek plans to form an alliance with his former enemies, break with the Communists, and massacre the militants. The leadership of the International and Chinese Communist Party decide that they are too weak to engage in the struggle and forbid any revolutionary action. They allow Chiang Kai-shek a free hand, in the hope that this timorous attitude will lead Chiang to think that repression of the Communists is pointless and to maintain his previous policy, or, at least, to postpone the break with them.

The Shanghai militants, who are already fully engaged in action, are rightly convinced of the contrary. For material as well as ideological reasons, however, they cannot act in isolation and in opposition to the Party leadership. So they are left with no option but to face defeat and massacre. The novel recounts their action just prior to the entry of the Kuomintang into Shanghai, their reactions on learning the decisions of the Party leadership, their defeat after Chiang Kai-shek's entry into the city and, lastly, the torture and massacre of the Communists by Chiang's men—a massacre in which, among many others, two of the novel's three heroes, Kyo and Katow, are killed.

The work begins with a famous scene: Chen's assassination of an arms dealer, or, to be more precise, an agent, in order to get from him a document that will enable the revolutionaries to gain possession of a number of pistols. This assassination reveals at once the difference between Chen and Hong: on the psychological plane, it is an act that will help Chen to become aware of his personal problems; on the material level, it is an act ordered by the revolutionary *organization* and therefore forms part of an *organized* action. There is a passage in the book that indicates both the importance of this assassination for the collective struggle and the particular meaning it has for Chen himself:

> The approaching attempt to place Shanghai in the hands of the revolutionaries would not have two hundred rifles behind it. If the short carbines (almost three hundred in number) which the dead entrepreneur had just arranged to sell the Government were thrown in too, the chances of the rebels would be doubled, for their first step would be to seize the arms of the police for their own troops. But during the last ten minutes, Chen had not once thought about that.

Having carried out the murder, Chen has to walk through the hotel, where life continues its usual way. The episode leads to a remarkable description of the opposition between two qualitatively different worlds: that of revolutionary action and that of an everyday life indifferent to ideas and politics. In *La Condition humaine,* this opposition serves to indicate Chen's awareness of the difference between the world of terrorist action to which he belongs and that of "the life of men who do not kill." Some years later, in *Les Noyers de l'Altenburg,* Malraux was to use a similar description to indicate Victor Berger's discovery, in Marseilles, at the time he was abandoning the struggle for the victory of *Ottomanism* (for which, I believe, one should read *Communism*), of the existence of the world of everyday life that is indifferent to ideas and action, in which however unattached he may be, he fails to become integrated. Chen, meeting a "Burmese or Siamese by the look of him, and rather drunk," who says to him "the little piece in red is an absolute peach!", wanted "both to strike him, to make him hold his tongue, and to embrace him because he was alive." In *Les Noyers de l'Altenburg,* only the opposition between the two worlds, that of action and that of everyday life, is emphasized. In *La Condition humaine,* on the other hand, there is added, by way of opposition, to the everyday life that is indifferent to politics and the world of terrorist action that isolates, a third world whose development constitutes the essential subject of the novel: that of the revolutionary community, to which Chen's action partly belongs and whose function and aim are precisely to integrate the two others. After the murder of the agent and the walk through the hotel full of indifferent merrymakers, Chen returns to his comrades:

> Their presence was breaking down Chen's ghastly feeling of isolation. It yielded gently, like an uprooted plant which still clings to the ground with a few slender threads. And as he gradually drew nearer to them it seemed to him that he suddenly knew them for the first time—as he had known his sister after his first visit to a brothel.

I have said that Chen corresponds much more to the character of Garine than to that of Hong and that, in the last resort, he is a synthesis of the two. As for Hong, his first assassination will be an intoxication, a decisive turning-point in his life. Like Garine, however, he will return after the assassination to the organization of revolutionary militants that Hong was never to see again, and never at any point in the novel does he come into opposition with that organization. Like Garine, too, he works within the collective struggle, but does not identify himself with it.

Having returned, after the assassination, to the group of revolutionaries, Chen meets among his comrades two characters who are at the centre of the novel, not so much as individuals, but as representatives of the entire group, of the revolutionary community—Katow and Kyo.

What characterizes each of them is their total commitment to action. In the book, Katow will be seen only as a militant in the struggle, at the moment of his arrest, then of his execution. Kyo, on the other hand, will be seen also in his private life, in his relations with May. But this does not represent the addition of a new, different sphere, for May and Kyo are characterized by the organic synthesis of their public and private lives, or, to use Lukács's expression, by the total synthesis of the individual and the citizen; and precisely because, in everyday life, this synthesis—which did not exist in Malraux's earlier writings either—is extremely rare, it is important to stress the extent to which Kyo's thinking and consciousness are *entirely* engaged in action. Moreover, Malraux will tell us on several occasions that Kyo's entire thinking was organically structured by the imminent struggle.

One such moment is when he is entering the Chinese quarter, after deciding to attack the boat and take the pistols:

> "A good quarter," thought Kyo. For more than a month he had gone from one meeting to another, organizing the rising, oblivious of the existence of streets: what was mud to him beside his plans? . . .
>
> As he turned out of a narrow passage he suddenly found himself looking down one of the main streets, wide and well-lit. Despite the rain beating down, which half obscured its outlines, he never for a moment saw it save as something flat which would have to be attacked in the face of rifles and machine-guns, firing horizontally.

Another moment occurs when he has crossed the Chinese quarter and reached the gates of the Concession:

> Two Annamese troopers and a sergeant from the Colonial army came and examined his papers. He had his French passport. As a temptation to the guards, hopeful Chinamen had stuck little pies all over the barbs of the wire. ("Good way of poisoning a station, if need be," thought Kyo.)

Once inside the Concession, he looks for Clappique. As I have already remarked, Clappique lives not in reality, but in imagination. This is expressed among other things by his external appearance: whatever he was wearing—tonight he was in evening clothes—Baron Clappique looked as if he were in disguise.

He finds him drawing an imaginary picture of Chiang Kai-shek for the benefit of two dancing-girls. How does he see himself in this picture?:

> "And what'll *you* find to do?"
>
> He whimpered: "Can't you guess, dear girl, do you mean to say you can't guess? I shall be Court astrologer, and one night when I am drunk—can it be tonight?—I shall meet my death digging for the moon in a pond!"

I shall come back later to the two other characters to be examined here—Gisors and Ferral.

What defines *La Condition humaine* in relation to the previous novels is first of all the absence of the element that was the most important in those works, the principal characteristic of Garine, Perken, and even Borodin—illness. Illness does exist, of course, in *La Condition humaine,* but only to the extent that the work *also* is in part a social chronicle: illness among the children of the poor, the consequences of an unsuccessful suicide attempt by a woman who wanted to die in order to avoid being married to a rich old man, etc. As revolutionary militants, the heroes themselves may be massacred and tortured, but they remain nevertheless essentially healthy; one might even go so far as to say that they define, by their existence, the summit of the human condition and, therefore, the summit of health. If there is disease, it concerns, not the individuals, but the revolutionary collectivity that is the true hero of the novel and whose problematic character I have already remarked on. It would not be possible here to study the psychology of this community step by step, so we shall approach it from two particularly important points of view: love and death, the relations between Kyo and May on the one hand, and, on the other, the torture and execution of the revolutionaries after Chiang Kai-shek's victory.

Love and death are, in effect, two important elements in characterizing fictional characters in general and particularly those of Malraux. In *La Condition humaine,* however, they have a different nature and function from those that they had in the previous works. I have already said that, in Malraux's world, relations between men and women always reflect the overall relation between men and the world. That is why, in the world of Perken and Garine, we met only eroticism and relations of domination, whereas in *La Condition humaine,* a novel of the authentic revolutionary community, eroticism is, like the individual, integrated and superseded in an authentic, higher community: that of love.

In *La Voie royale* one sentence alone hinted at the possibility of the relation that was to be at the centre of *La Condition humaine.* I have already quoted it: at the moment when Perken, learning of his imminent death, takes refuge in a final erotic fling, at the moment he becomes aware of the impossibility of any lasting erotic possession, he also realizes that "one possesses only what one loves."

These words, *which have no meaning in the world of La Voie royale, where love is nonexistent,* prefigure *La Condition humaine,* in which Malraux was to create with Kyo and May the first pair of lovers in his *oeuvre* and one of the most beautiful, purest love stories in major twentieth-century fiction.

Eroticism and domination are not, of course, totally absent from the work—there are even justly famous scenes of this kind, but they involve, not Kyo and May, the heroes of the novel, but the subsidiary character of Ferral, who as I have already said, corresponds in certain respects to Garine/Perken. In addition, though in a more human context, we also find in the character of Chen, who is also to a large degree reminiscent of Garine, the same pure erotic relationship with women.

However, between the eroticism and domination of the previous novels and the same relations in *La Condition humaine,* there is an important difference—one that is essential for the understanding of the characters. In the earlier novels, eroticism and domination constituted precarious, but positive values, whereas they are entirely modified, even devalued by the very presence of love in this novel of the revolutionary community. I shall return to this. Let us begin however with the love of Kyo and May which is, in *La Condition humaine,* a story of love in the twentieth century, a period in which such a feeling is no longer accessible to every man or woman. That is why it can be successful only in so far as it is organically linked to the revolutionary action of the two partners.

The story of this love is that of an entirely new feeling that comes into conflict with the relics that still exist in each of them of a type of feeling and eroticism that they have in fact superseded. In other words, Kyo and May cannot always live up to their own existence and the weakness that survives in each of them will finally be overcome only through action and imminent death, which help them and force them to rediscover their own levels.

The facts are well known: knowing that their relationship allows each of them both to preserve his own freedom and to respect the freedom of the other, May in a moment of exhaustion—and, partly also, moved by the pity and solidarity that binds her to a man who she knows will run the risk of being killed in a few hours—has slept with a comrade, even though she did not love him. Convinced that this is of no importance in her relations with Kyo, which on the contrary would be affected by the slightest lie, she tells Kyo about it. Kyo feels intense pain and an acute feeling of jealousy:

> Kyo felt pain in its most degrading form; pain which his self-respect dare not admit. In point of fact she was free to sleep with whoever she wished. What then was the cause of his suffering for which he could find no justification, but which held him in such complete subjection? . . .
>
> "Kyo, I'm going to tell you something strange, but true. Until five minutes ago, I thought you wouldn't mind. Perhaps it suited me to think so. There are some things people ask of one, above all when death is as near as this (it's other people's death that I've had to face till now, Kyo . . .) which have no connexion with love. . . ."
>
> Jealousy there was, notwithstanding; all the less clearly perceived in that the desire which she awoke in him was based upon affection. His eyes closed, and, still leaning on his elbow, he set himself the painful task of understanding. He could hear nothing but May's laboured breathing and the scratching of the puppy's paws. The principal cause of his suffering (he would inevitably find others: he could feel them lying in ambush, like his comrades who still waited behind their closed doors) lay in his idea that that man who had just slept with May ("I can't after all call him her lover") despised her. The man in question was an old friend of hers, whom he hardly knew; but he knew well enough the contempt in which women were ultimately held by almost all men. "The idea that having slept with her, as a result of having slept with her, he may be thinking: 'That little tart'; I could kill him for that. Are we always only jealous of what we imagine the other person is thinking? Men are pretty hopeless creatures. . . ." As far as May was concerned, sexual relations implied no kind of contract. That ought to be made clear to this man. If he slept with her, well and good; but don't let him start thinking he possessed her. ("This is becoming pitiable. . . .") But that was something out of his control—and he knew that, in any case, it wasn't the vital thing. The vital thing, the thing which was torturing him almost beyond endurance, was the barrier

which had suddenly cut him off from her: it wasn't hatred which had done it, though there was hatred in him: it wasn't jealousy (or perhaps that was just what jealousy was?): it was a feeling to which he could give no name, as destructive as Time or Death: he could not recapture her.

And Kyo leaves without relations between them returning to normal:

May offered him her lips. In his heart Kyo wanted to kiss her; not her mouth, though—as if there alone bitterness still lingered. He kissed her at last, clumsily. She looked at him sadly, with listless eyes which suddenly filled with animation as the muscles regained control. He left her.

It is only when he is alone in the street again, involved once more in action, that he realizes how deep their love is:

"What have other men in common with me? Just so many entities who look at me and criticize. My real fellow-creatures love me unreflectingly, love me in spite of everything, love me so that no corruption, vileness or betrayal has any power to alter it: love me for myself and not for what I have done or will do; whose love for me goes as far as my own—embracing suicide. . . . With her alone do I share a love like that, whatever batterings it may have undergone, as others share the sickness of their children, their risk of death . . ." It certainly wasn't a feeling of happiness, it was something primeval, in tune with the darkness, which set him tingling till he stood there locked in an embrace, as if his cheek were laid against another—the only part of him which was stronger than death.
On the roof-tops, vague shapes were already at their posts.

The crisis is overcome only at the moment of defeat, when Kyo sets out for the meeting of the Central Committee; he knows, as does May, that he will probably be arrested and executed. At first, however, the tension seems to accumulate:

"Where are you going?"
"With you, Kyo."
"What for?"
There was no reply.

"We shall be more easily recognized together than separately," he said.

"I don't see why. If you're on their list, nothing is going to make any difference. . . ."

"You can't do any good."

"What good should I do waiting here? Men don't know what waiting is like."

He walked a few steps, then stopped and turned towards her.

"Listen, May: when it was a question of your freedom, I gave it you."

She knew what he was alluding to, and it frightened her: she had forgotten it. She was right, for he went on, dully this time:

". . . and you took advantage of it all right. Now it's mine that is involved."

"But, Kyo, what has that got to do with it?"

"To recognize someone else's right to liberty is to acknowledge that that is more important than one's own suffering: I know that from experience."

"Am I just 'someone else,' Kyo?"

He remained silent. Yes, at that moment, she was. A change had taken place in their relations.

"You mean that because I . . . well, because of that, in future we can't even face danger together? Think, Kyo: one would almost imagine this was a kind of revenge."

"Not to be able to any more and to try to when it's useless are quite different things."

"But if it rankled as much as that, you could perfectly well have taken a mistress. At least, no: that's not true. Why do I say that? I didn't take a lover, I just went to bed with somebody. It's not the same thing, and you know quite well that you can sleep with anyone you want."

"I'm satisfied with you," he answered bitterly.

May was rather puzzled by the way he looked at her. Every possible feeling seemed to enter into his expression. What made her feel really uneasy was the quite unconscious lust which was apparent in his face.

"As far as that goes," he went on, "my feelings are the same now as they were a fortnight ago: I just don't want to. I'm not saying that you are wrong, but that I want to go alone. You acknowledge my liberty; you possess the same degree of liberty yourself. Liberty to do what *you* please. Liberty isn't a bargain, it's just liberty."

"It's a desertion."

Silence.

"What is it that brings people who love each other to face death, unless it is that they can face it together?"

She guessed that he was going to leave without further argument, and placed herself in front of the door.

"You shouldn't have given me this liberty, if we have to be separated now as a result."

"You certainly didn't ask for it."

"You had already given it me."

"You shouldn't have believed me," he thought. It was true, he had always given it. But that she should discuss rights now, that widened the gulf between them.

"There are some rights which one only grants," she said bitterly, "so that they shall not be used."

"If they had been granted so that you could hang on to them at this moment it wouldn't be so bad . . ."

In that second they were drawing even farther apart than in death. Eyelids, mouth, temples, a dead woman's face still shows the site of every caress, whereas those high cheekbones and elongated eyelids which confronted him then belonged to a foreign world. The wounds of the deepest love suffice to create a thorough hatred. Was she so near death that she was recoiling from the animosity which she had seen preparing? She said:

"I'm not hanging on to anything, Kyo. Say I am making a mistake if you like, that I've already made one; say what you please, but just at this moment I want to go with you; now, at once. I beg you."

He didn't answer.

"If you didn't love me," she went on, "you wouldn't think twice about letting me come. Well then? Why cause us unnecessary suffering?"

"As if this were a good time to choose," she added wearily . . .

"Are we going?" she asked.

"No."

Too honest to hide her impulses, she reiterated her desires with a cat-like persistence which often exasperated Kyo. She had moved away from the door, but he realized that all the time he had wanted to pass through he had been sure that he wouldn't really do it.

"May, are we just going to leave each other quite suddenly like this?"

"Have I behaved like a woman who expects protection?"

They stood there face to face, not knowing what else to say, and not content to remain silent, conscious at once that that moment was one of the most solemn of their lives, and that it could not endure—that time was already corrupting it: Kyo's place was not there, but with the Committee, and a certain impatience lurked all the time at the back of his mind.

She nodded towards the door.

He looked at her, took her head between his hands and drew it gently towards him, without kissing her; as though in that firm embrace he had somehow projected all the mingled tenderness and ardour of which masculine love is capable. At last he withdrew his hands.

The doors shut, one after the other. May continued to listen, as if she were expecting to hear a third one close, brought into existence by her imagination. Her mouth hanging limply open, wild with grief, she was beginning to realize that if she had signed to him to leave, it was because she saw in that movement the one final hope of persuading him to take her with him.

But, once in the street, Kyo again feels the strength that unites him to May:

Parting had not relieved Kyo's distress. The reverse was the case: May seemed all the stronger in this deserted street—after yielding to him—than when she had been fighting him face-to-face. He entered the Chinese town, aware of the fact, but quite indifferent to it. "Have I behaved like a woman who needs protection?" What right had he to extend his pitiable protection to this woman who had submitted even to his leaving her? *Why* was he leaving her? Was it perhaps a kind of vengeance? No doubt May was still sitting on the bed, broken by despair which no reasoning could alleviate.

He turned and ran back.

The phoenix-room was empty: his father had gone out, May was still where he had left her. He stopped in front of the door, overwhelmed by a feeling of the friendliness of death, and yet conscious of how, despite its fascination, his body recoiled grimly before the unnaturalness of the contact. He understood now that to be willing to lead the woman he loved to her death was perhaps love in its most complete form, the love beyond which nothing can go.

He opened the door.

Without a word she hurriedly threw her cloak around her shoulders, and followed him out.

When they arrive at the meetingplace, May is knocked unconscious and Kyo arrested. Later, when he's about to be executed, he swallows the cyanide that most of the revolutionary leaders carried with them for just such an eventuality, thus killing himself in order to avoid torture. At the moment of death, he rediscovers unreservedly, and in their entirety, both May and all his comrades in the struggle:

Kyo shut his eyes. . . . He had witnessed death on many occasions and, aided in this by his Japanese upbringing, he had always felt that it would be beautiful to die a death that is one's own, a death appropriate to the life it closes. And to die is passive, but to kill oneself is to turn passivity into action. As soon as they came to fetch the first of his lot, he would kill himself in full consciousness of what he was doing. He remembered the gramophone records and his heart dropped a beat: in those days hope still had meaning. He would never see May again, and the only hurt he felt was the hurt that she would feel—as if he were doing something unkind, and wrong, in dying. "Death brings remorse," he thought, with a twinge of irony. He felt no such qualms for his father, who had always given him an impression not of weakness, but of strength. For more than a year now May had protected him from all loneliness, though not from every sorrow. There sprang into his mind, alas, as soon as he thought of her, the remembrance of that swift refuge in tenderness of body joined to body. Now that he was no longer to be numbered among the living. . . . "She will have to forget me now." Could he have written to tell her so, he would only have been torturing her and tying her closer to him. "And it would mean telling her to love another. . . ." Oh, this prison— a place where time stops still, while elsewhere it runs on.

Compared with this total union between Kyo and May, in which one can dissociate in no way the private relationship from the revolutionary activity, compared with this *realized totality,* the other relationship between man and woman described in the novel, that between Ferral and Valérie (there are only a few references to Chen's erotic relations with prostitutes) is naturally devalued and degraded; and it is hardly surprising if this devaluation necessarily involves in *La Condition humaine* a change of nature. There is no longer any domination, any predominance on the part of the man. Valérie revolts and, in order to humiliate Ferral, arranges to meet him in the hotel lounge at the same time as another meeting she has arranged with a character of the same world—each man having been instructed to bring a canary. Valérie does not turn up at the rendezvous and the two men find themselves face to face, ridiculous, accompanied by their servants carrying the cages with the birds.

By way of revenge, Ferral fills Valérie's room with birds. We do not know what happens afterwards—and we hardly care. The relationship has lost all interest.

And yet, in *Les Conquérants* and *La Voie royale,* this relationship of erotic domination was, on the level of the private life, the very value that enabled Garine and Perken to assert themselves and to feel their own existence.

In addition to love, death is the other event that constitutes the existence of the main characters in the novel. In my comments on the moment when Kyo swallows the cyanide and feels May's presence in an unusually intense way, I pointed out the significance and function that death has for the revolutionaries of *La Condition humaine,* a significance and function different and even opposed to those that it had for Garine and Perken in the earlier novels. In *Les Conquérants* and *La Voie royale,* death was the inevitable reality that rendered precarious and provisional all social values bound up with action, which annihilated them *retroactively* and brought the hero back to the formless, to absolute solitude, whereas in *La Condition humaine* it is, on the contrary, the moment that realizes in its entirety an organic union with action and a community with the other comrades. In the preceding novels death broke all links between the individual and the community. In *La Condition humaine* it ensures the final supersession of solitude. Among the characters embodying the revolutionary group itself, two deaths have already been described for us, those of Katow and Kyo. I have already spoken of the latter: Kyo is to die, reunited not only with May, but also with Katow, his comrades, and above all the very meaning of his struggle and his existence. That is why his death is not an end: his life and his struggle will be taken up again by all those who continue the action after him:

He would die having fought for what in his own day would
have possessed the strongest meaning and inspired the most
splendid hope; die, too, among those whom he would wish to
have seen live; die, like each of these recumbent forms, so as to
give significance to his own life. What would have been the
value of a life for which he would not have accepted death? It
is less hard to die when one is not alone in dying. This death of
his was hallowed by a touch of common brotherhood, by contact
with a gathering of broken men whom future multitudes would
recognize as martyrs, whose bloody memory would bring forth
a golden hope! How, already staring into the eyes of death,
should he fail to hear the murmur of human sacrifice calling
aloud to him that the heart of man is a resting-place for the dead,
well worth the loss of life itself? . . .

No, dying could become an action, an exalted deed, the supreme expression of a life to which this death was itself so similar;
it meant, too, escape from these two soldiers who now uncer-
tainly approached him. He jerked the poison between his teeth,
as he would have barked an order, heard anguished Katow still
asking him something, felt him stir and touch him; then just as,
gasping for breath, he tried to clutch him, he felt his whole
strength slip, fading from him, giving way before the onrush
of an overwhelming convulsion.

Similarly, Katow's death is the moment at which he is reunited in the
most intense way with the revolutionary community. Beside him, two
Chinese militants are lying full length, terrified by the whistle of the locomotive into which Chiang Kai-shek has the prisoners thrown alive. Katow, in an act of supreme fraternity, gives them his cyanide. Unfortunately,
one of the Chinese is wounded in the hand and drops it. For a few moments
it might be thought that Katow's act had no efficacity. But beyond the
material reality, fraternity is stronger and more present than ever. His two
Chinese comrades no longer feel alone:

Their hands brushed against his. Then suddenly one of these
hands seized his hand, clutched it, held it fast.
"Even if we don't find anything," said one of the voices,
"still. . . ."

But the cyanide is found again, and his two comrades escape torture.
Katow is led to the train. It is perhaps the most intense and solemn moment
in the novel. He goes through the scene surrounded by the fraternity of all

the other prisoners, wounded, bound to the ground, and destined to the same fate:

The torch-flare now showed him in even blacker silhouette against the windows that looked out on to the night. He walked heavily, slumping first on one leg, then the other, hampered by his wounds; as he staggered towards the glare of the torch, the shadowed outline of his head merged into the roof. The entire darkness of the hall had come to life and watched him step by step. The silence now was such that the ground rang at each heavy tread of his foot. Nodding up and down, every head followed the rhythm of his walk, tenderly, in terror, in resignation, as if, although all the movements were the same, each man would himself have struggled to follow these faltering footsteps. No head fell back as the door closed.

A sound of deep breathing, like the sound of sleep, came up from the ground; breathing through the nose, jaws clenched in anguish, not stirring now, quite still, all those who were not yet dead waited to hear the shriek of a distant whistle.

It becomes obvious that the subject of *La Condition humaine* is not only a chronicle of the events in Shanghai; it is also, indeed primarily, this extraordinary realization of the revolutionary community in the defeat of the militants and their survival in the revolutionary struggle that continues after their death. And, of course, it is in relation to this struggle that the later destiny of the other characters is situated. Two of them, Hemmelrich and Chen, will be brought back into the struggle. The former had hesitated all his life between his duties to his wife and child, passive victims, incapable of defending themselves in a barbarous and unjust world, and his revolutionary aspirations; he will be freed by the repression which, murdering those dearest to him, gives him back the freedom he had always dreamed of and enables him to commit himself entirely to action.

Chen, who was supported unofficially by the group of revolutionaries, tried twice to organize an assassination attempt on Chiang Kai-shek. He is cut to shreds during the second attempt and kills himself. At the moment he throws the bomb, he finds himself entirely alone and when he dies he is aware that in this world "even the death of Chiang Kai-shek can no longer affect him." This is, on the immediate level, the death of Garine and Perken, but at the end of the novel we learn that his disciple Pei, through whom he had hoped to ensure the continuity of his anarchist action, has set out for Russia and joined the communists. Thus Chen's very act and total solitude into which he found himself thrown back at the moment of death have been superseded and integrated by historical action.

Three characters leave the orbit of action: Gisors, for whom Kyo's death broke all links with the revolution, returns to the passive pantheism of traditional Chinese culture; Ferral is ousted from action by a consortium of bankers and civil servants who take over his work; Clappique is forced to hide from the repression that is directed at him insofar as he helped Kyo and disguises himself as a sailor—a disguise in which he finds the true meaning of his life.

There remain the combatants, May, and, behind her, Pei and Hemmelrich, about whom something more should be said. The novel tells us simply that all three went to the USSR, where they continue the struggle, and that they will later come back to China, the construction of the USSR, the realization of the five-year plan having become "the main weapon of the class struggle" for the moment.

Malraux's ideological position at the time he wrote the novel, therefore, was not Trotskyist, but, on the contrary, fairly close to the Stalinist positions. Nevertheless, the two chapters that express his position, namely the twenty-odd pages of part 3 that take place in Hankow, and the last six pages of the book, are much more abstract and schematic than the rest of the novel, and appear to some extent as an afterthought or foreign body.

If the unity of the novel does not suffer from this, and if *La Condition humaine* remains a powerfully coherent and unified novel, it is above all because these fragments scarcely add up to a tenth of the work; moreover this tenth is not entirely devoted to expressing this ideological position.

In fact, Malraux's explicit ideology has an insignificant place in *La Condition humaine,* whereas the unorthodox point of view of the Shanghai revolutionaries constitutes the unifying point of view from which the novel is written. Nevertheless, in each of these two passages, Malraux is forced to make the transition between two almost irreconcilable positions. He does this in the chapter that takes place in Hankow by referring to "all the hesitations" of Vologuin, the representative of the International. These doubts are expressed in the fact that, while declaring himself to be opposed to any assassination attempt on individuals, and in particular against the attempt on Chiang Kai-shek proposed by Chen, Vologuin nevertheless lets Chen go, thus encouraging his terrorist action.

Malraux also makes this transition at the end of the work in the psychology of May who, going over to the side of the Party and the International, becomes integrated in a struggle that must in principle absorb and integrate that of the Shanghai revolutionaries. May is going, we are led to believe, to begin a new life, but she does so "without enthusiasm," with a heavy heart and, quite obviously, without having resolved her problems: " 'I hardly ever weep now, any more,' she said with bitter pride."

In *Les Conquérants* and *La Condition humaine*, Malraux wrote the first two French novels of the proletarian revolution of the twentieth century. He did not identify himself, however, with the Communist Party that directed this revolution. Indeed, we have seen that the fundamental values that structure the worlds of these two works are different from those of the Party, although the Party represented, in each case, a positive value and, quite obviously the transition from the novel of Garine to that of the community of the Shanghai revolutionaries constitutes an important step towards a revolutionary perspective.

This study had already been published when I realized that, in *L'Etre et le néant*, Sartre develops against Heidegger and against Malraux (to whom he attributes only the position of *L'Espoir* according to which "death transforms life into destiny") an analysis very close to the one I developed in studying *Les Conquérants* and *La Voie royale*. No doubt, historical action enjoys no privilege in this radically individualistic work but, for Sartre, man defines himself by the fundamental project and the secondary projects that attach themselves to it, in the perspective of which the death to come is not a possibility of the subject but, on the contrary, an external given, an unforeseen, unexpected hindrance, which he must take into account, by preserving in it its specifically unexpected character. Thus these projects deprive the consciousness of death of any decisive importance until the day inevitable death destroys *retroactively* the value of these projects.

Excluding any conscious influence, the fact that two writers of this importance should develop in France, at so short a distance in time, positions so complex and so similar leads one to suspect the action of trans-individual and probably social action; but for the moment this observation simply poses a problem and I have no hypothesis that might help me to elucidate it.

Kyo and "La Fraternité Virile"

C. J. Greshoff

It seems likely that Malraux saw in Kyo the protagonist of his novel. We have seen [elsewhere] however that this dominant role in the novel has been partly usurped by Tchen. Kyo is nevertheless important and the two characters are closely linked: *La Condition humaine* is to a great extent, the novel of the two half-brothers Tchen and Kyo.

Like so many of Malraux's heroes, Kyo has a mixed background: he is half-Chinese, half-Japanese. His early years were spent in Japan, the later in China. There are good reasons for giving his protagonists such mixed backgrounds. One we have already pointed out being tragic heroes they belong nowhere. But the mixed nature of their origin and background serves also to emphasize that they are not the products of a background, the children of their childhood; they have no childhood. They are rootless and therefore they are not what they have become, but what they have done and do: Perken *is* his adventure, Garine *is* his action, and Kyo *is* his revolutionary action. In this way Kyo is a simple character: "Les questions individuelles ne se posaient pour Kyo que dans sa vie privée." So we are shown two Kyos: the simple Kyo who lives his public revolutionary life and the Kyo who lives a much more complex private life. The first one obviously holds little interest for the novelist for the simple reason that individual problems do not arise in his relationship with the revolution and the Party. He is totally at one with them, he serves the cause with a total devotion so that his individuality is, as it were, dissolved in the communal

From *An Introduction to the Novels of André Malraux.* © 1975 by C. J. Greshoff. A. A. Balkema, 1975.

action. It is significant that in contrast to Tchen who because of personal problems is pushed into political action, Kyo *chooses* his political action:

> Ici Gisors retrouvait son fils, indifférent au christianisme mais à qui l'éducation japonaise (Kyo avait vécu au Japon de sa huitième à sa dix-septième année) avait imposé aussi la conviction que les idées ne devaient pas être pensées, mais vécues. Kyo avait choisi l'action, d'une façon grave et préméditée, comme d'autres choisissent les armes ou la mer: il avait quitté son père, vécu à Canton, à Tientsin, de la vie des manoeuvres et des coolies-pousse, pour organiser les syndicats.

There is in Kyo's decision, a determination which is totally lacking in Tchen's. The words which describe Tchen's engagement: "Tout le précipitait à l'action politique" suggest a sort of blind urgency. He is being thrown into the revolution, admittedly not against his will but neither because he wills it. Moreover Kyo is quite clear about what he wants, what he is fighting for:

> Il n'était pas inquiet. Sa vie avait un sens, et il le connaissait: donner à chacun de ces hommes que la famine, en ce moment même, faisait mourir comme une peste lente, la possession de sa propre dignité. Il n'y a pas de dignité possible, pas de vie réelle pour un homme qui travaille douze heures par jour sans savoir pour quoi il travaille. Il fallait que ce travail prît un sens, devînt une patrie.

Much later, after his arrest, he explains to the police chief König why he is a communist:

> —On m'a dit que vous êtes communiste par . . . Comment, déjà? dignité. C'est vrai? . . .
> —Je pense que le communisme rendra la dignité possible pour ceux avec qui je combats. Ce qui est contre lui, en tout cas, les contraint à n'en pas avoir.

What comes through in both these quotations is a kind of quiet, objective altruism which stands again in strong contrast to Tchen's very subjective motivation. "L'espoir d'un monde différent" is vague and is significantly mixed with "la satisfaction de *ses* haines, de *sa* pensée, de *son* caractère" (my emphasis). Finally, in contrast to the solitary and isolated Tchen who at the height of the revolutionary struggle feels cut off from his comrades ("Il n'était pas des leurs"), Kyo is completely at one with them:

Il était des leurs: ils avaient les mêmes ennemis. Métis, hors-caste, dédaigné des Blancs et plus encore des Blanches, Kyo n'avait pas tenté de les séduire: il avait cherché les siens et les avait trouvés.

Kyo fights *with* his comrades and he will die with them. Tchen dies alone an ironically useless death (Chiang Kai-shek is not killed) and he dies in a cruel messy way which is described in a very detached manner:

> On s'approchait. Il se souvint qu'il devait prendre son revolver. Il tenta d'atteindre sa poche de pantalon. Plus de poche, plus de pantalon, plus de jambe: de la chair hachée. . . . Il ouvrit enfin les yeux. Tout tournait, d'une façon lente et invincible, selon un très grand cercle, et pourtant rien n'existait que la douleur. Un policier était tout près. Tchen voulut demander si Chiang-Kai-Shek était mort, mais il voulait cela dans un autre monde; dans ce monde-ci, cette mort même lui était indifférente.
>
> De toute sa force, le policier le retourna d'un coup de pied dans les côtes. Tchen hurla, tira en avant, au hasard, et la secousse rendit plus intense encore cette douleur qu'il croyait sans fond. Il allait s'évanouir ou mourir. Il fit le plus terrible effort de sa vie, parvint à introduire dans sa bouche le canon du revolver. Prévoyant la nouvelle secousse, plus douloureuse encore que la précédente, il ne bougeait plus. Un furieux coup de talon d'un autre policier crispa tous ses muscles: il tira sans s'en apercevoir.

Kyo on the other hand dies surrounded by his comrades; he dies, as it were, a fertile death to which, significantly, Malraux gives lyrical expression:

> Pourtant, la fatalité acceptée par eux montait avec leur bourdonnement de blessés comme la paix du soir, recouvrait Kyo, ses yeux fermés, ses mains croisées sur son corps abandonné, avec une majesté de chant funèbre. Il aurait combattu pour ce qui, de son temps, aurait été chargé du sens le plus fort et du plus grand espoir; il mourrait parmi ceux avec qui il aurait voulu vivre; il mourrait, comme chacun de ces hommes couchés, pour avoir donné un sens à sa vie. Qu'eût valu une vie pour laquelle il n'eût pas accepté de mourir? Il est facile de mourir quand on ne meurt pas seul. Mort saturée de ce chevrotement fraternel, assemblée de vaincus où des multitudes reconnaîtraient leurs martyrs, légende sanglante dont se font les légendes dorées! Comment, déjà regardé par la mort, ne pas entendre ce murmure

de sacrifice humain qui lui criait que le coeur viril des hommes
est un refuge à morts qui vaut bien l'esprit?

Let us first consider Kyo, the revolutionary, since it is he whom we meet
first at Hemmelrich's record shop where Tchen goes after the murder. Kyo,
the man of action, is almost always in company with Katow, and Katow
is the dominant person: it is he, for instance, who instructs the *groupes de
combat* how to destroy tanks, it is he who leads the raid on the ammunition-
carrying cargo boat. It is obvious that Katow is older and much more
experienced than Kyo. This dominance of Katow over Kyo helps also to
establish a contrast between Katow, the real professional revolutionary
whose entire life is lived in the revolution and Kyo, who in spite of his
dedication, has nevertheless another life which does not belong to the revolution. The fact that "les questions individuelles ne se posaient que dans
sa vie privée" shows that unlike Katow, he *has* individual problems and
that he has a private life which is kept separate from his revolutionary life;
Kyo is by no means a middle-class young man who "plays" at being a
revolutionary but he is not either in the class of the true professional revolutionaries such as Borodin or the fictional Katow.

In the scene where we meet Kyo for the first time, Malraux has placed
one of the key images of the novel. Some recordings of Kyo's voice had
been made; now in Hemmelrich's shop he is listening to the playback, but
does not recognise his own voice. The meaning of the experience is grad-
ually made clear. First the purely physiological phenomenon is explained
("C'est sans doute une question de moyens: nous entendons la voix des
autres avec les oreilles. Et la nôtre avec la gorge"). It acquires its deeper
symbolic meaning in two parallel meditations of Gisors and Kyo. To both
the episode of the records comes back to mind after a crucial experience.
Kyo thinks about it when he has heard that May went to bed with another
man: Gisors, after Tchen's confession, when he discovers that he cannot
really understand Tchen. To both the experience acquires the same meaning:
it illustrates the utter isolation of each man:

> (Kyo) s'enfonçait en lui-même comme dans cette ruelle de plus
> en plus noire, où même les isolateurs du télégraphe ne luisaient
> plus sur le ciel. Il y retrouvait l'angoisse, et se souvint des disques:
> 'On entend la voix des autres avec ses oreilles, la sienne avec la
> gorge.' Oui. Sa vie aussi, on l'entend avec la gorge, et celle des
> autres? . . . Il y avait d'abord la solitude, la solitude immuable
> derrière la multitude mortelle comme la grande nuit primitive

derrière cette nuit dense et basse sous quoi guettait la ville déserte, pleine d'espoir et de haine.

And Gisors:

Comme Kyo, et presque pour les mêmes raisons, il songea aux disques dont celui-ci lui avait parlé, et presque de la même façon, car les modes de pensée de Kyo étaient nés des siens. De même que Kyo n'avait pas reconnu sa propre voix parce qu'il l'avait entendue avec la gorge, de même la conscience que lui, Gisors, prenait de lui-même, était sans doute irréductible à celle qu'il pouvait prendre d'un autre être, parce qu'elle n'était pas acquise par les mêmes moyens.

It is when we leave the world of action and see Kyo and May together that we enter into the world of the *questions individuelles* which, from the novelist's point of view whether he wants to or not, is the only valid world. We do not see him now engaged in action but we see him feeling, meditating: we get inside Kyo.

The relationship between Kyo and May is of great importance in making clear one of the meanings of the novel. Kyo without May would not have come face to face with his human condition. He would have fought and died in a world without anguish and without problems. ("Il n'était pas inquiet. Sa vie avait un sens, il le connaissait.") It is through May that suffering and anxiety come into Kyo's life and this anxiety will grow into a form of metaphysical *angst*. It is also with the couple Kyo-May that love, almost the only time, finds its place in the world of Malraux. A love devoid of sentimentality, almost devoid of words, those vehicles of sentimentality. In Malraux's world the language of affection and endearments is reserved for dogs and children. (May talking to her Pekinese: "chien velu, chien moussu, chien touffu." And Kassner's wife in *Le Temps du mépris* talking to her child: "Mon petit printemps, bouchonnet, poussin.") The affection which exists between May and Kyo is nevertheless very real: in a sense it is so real and profound that it need not be expressed. Yet the nonverbal, nonsentimental quality of their feelings comes also from the fact that their love has a kind of toughness which somehow is not wholly convincing but which brings it very close to the *fraternité virile*. This is accentuated by the virile characteristics which Malraux has given May: "May entra, son manteau de cuir bleu, d'une coupe presque militaire, accentuait ce qu'il y'avait de viril dans sa marche et même dans sa démarche." Yet in spite of their deep affection, in spite of this "entente charnelle entre eux," they both retain their sexual freedom. This is, of course, very much in keeping with the then current ethos of the communist intelligentsia. It is the exercise of this freedom by May that sparks off Kyo's personal crisis. When May tells Kyo casually: "Il faut que je te dise quelque chose qui va peut-être un peu t'embêter. . . . J'ai fini par coucher avec Lenglen, cet après-mid," Kyo's reactions are first of a psychological nature—hurt and bitterness, and pain at the thought of Lenglen's possible contempt for May: "L'idée qu'ayant couché avec elle . . . il peut penser d'elle: 'cette petite poule' me donne envie de l'assommer." But the reaction reaches deeper levels and finally reveals to Kyo his and Man's total solitude: "La solitude immuable derrière la multitude mortelle."

Just before he dies, Kyo's thoughts turn to May: "Depuis plus d'un an May l'avait délivré de toute solitude." Now what is important is that after May tells Kyo she went to bed with Lenglen, May in a very real sense dies for Kyo:

> Rien, pourtant, ne prévalait contre la décoloration de ce visage enseveli au fond de leur vie commune comme dans la brume, comme dans la terre. Il se souvint d'un ami qui avait vu mourir l'intelligence de la femme qu'il aimait, paralysée pendant des mois; il lui semblait voir mourir May ainsi, voir disparaître absurdement, comme un nuage qui se résorbe dans le ciel gris, la forme de son bonheur. Comme si elle fût morte deux fois, du temps, et de ce qu'elle lui disait.

And again more explicitly:

> L'essentiel, ce qui le troublait jusqu'à l'angoisse, c'est qu'il était tout à coup séparé d'elle, non par la haine—bien qu'il y eût de la haine en lui—non par la jalousie (ou bien la jalousie était-elle précisément cela?); par un sentiment sans nom, aussi destructeur que le temps ou la mort: il ne la retrouvait pas.

With this "death" of May disappears also the person who had freed Kyo from solitude: now he becomes suddenly and profoundly aware of this solitude. It is at this stage that Kyo discovers the true meaning of his strange experience when listening to the reproduction of his own voice.

Towards the end of the novel Kyo and May are reunited. When Chiang Kai-shek is preparing to crush the Communist Party, Kyo goes off to join his comrades and also goes towards his almost certain death. May wants to accompany him but Kyo, out of vengeance, refuses her the right to share his death with him. He leaves alone, yet "he comes back for her . . . offering as a complete token of love his willingness to lead her to death." Seen in this light the scene has, as we shall see, a certain resemblance to the scene where Katow shares his cyanide with his two comrades.

At the antipodes of Kyo we find the minor character Hemmelrich who in the organisation of the novel has nevertheless a certain importance. His function is linked to the dichotomy dignity/humiliation which is so important in the characterisation of Kyo. If Kyo is dignity, Hemmelrich is humiliation. There is a close resemblance between Rebecci in *Les Conquérants* and Hemmelrich. Rebecci is obviously a preliminary sketch. The young Italian anarchist who, defeated by poverty and life, now sells mechanical toys in Saigon, becomes a Belgian (with a strangely German sounding name) with a background of poverty: "d'un bout à l'autre (son souvenir) n'était que misère." He drifts to Shangai where he marries a Chinese woman: "qui s'était accrochée à lui d'un amour aveugle de chien martyrisé, soupçonnant qu'il était un autre chien martyrisé." He has a child who when the novel opens is dying. The misery and miserableness of Hemmelrich is a little overstressed which makes him not quite convincing as a character. One feels that Malraux is ill at ease with him, partly because he is not an intellectual who verbalises his predicament but an instinctive *révolté* in rebellion against the poverty and the humiliation to which he is condemned. Moreover his family obligations (he is the only character in *La Condition humaine* who has a family) rob him of his freedom and he cannot join his comrades in action which is another source of humiliation. Eventually Hemmelrich will be set free. When Chiang Kai-shek moves against the communists, Hemmelrich's record shop which had been a communist meeting place is "nettoyée à la grenade comme une tranchée," and his wife and ailing child are killed. The irony of the incident lies in the fact that for once death, the enemy, becomes an ally: "Pourtant, cette fois, la destinée avait mal joué: en lui arrachant tout ce qu'il possédait encore elle le libérait." The ironic accent in this sentence clearly falls on "cette fois." At the end of the novel Hemmelrich's life of poverty and humiliation is redeemed by working in the Soviet Union. "J'ai vu hier Hemmelrich," writes a co-refugee to May, "qui pense à vous. Il est monteur à l'usine d'électricité. Il m'a dit: 'c'est la première fois de ma vie que je travaille en sachant pourquoi, et non en attendant patiemment de crever.' " This redemption of Hemmelrich through Communism is too edifying and too moralising to be convincing.

Katow, as we had already occasion to remark, is the true professional revolutionary. He might be seen as a more worked-out version of Borodin in *Les Conquérants*. Katow appears only in scenes of action. One of the most interesting of these is the defence of the Communist *permanence* by Katow and Hemmelrich. Its interest derives partly from the fact that it is the counterpoint of the attack on the police station at the beginning of the novel: the Revolution triumphant and the Revolution defeated. The scene is also interesting because it reveals so clearly the resemblance of the world of Malraux with the world of the romanticised, melodramatic war pictures of the nineteenth century, for what we have in this scene of the last stand of Katow is a modernized version of the well-known *pompier* picture of the Franco-Prussian war: "Les Dernières cartouches."

Katow has been equipped by Malraux with a meagre and significantly, a purely political "biography":

> Katow condamné à cinq ans de bagne en 1905, lorsque, étudiant en médecine, il avait participé à l'attaque—puérile—de la prison d'Odessa. . . .
> Réfugié en Suisse de 1905 à 1912, date de son retour clandestin en Russie, il parlait français presque sans accent, mais en avalant un certain nombre de voyelles, comme s'il eût voulu compenser ainsi la nécessité d'articuler rigoureusement lorsqu'il parlait chinois.

The peculiarity of Katow's speech is not without interest. It is, as we have already seen, a rather artificial means of giving in the case of Katow some degree of individuality. The psychological content of Katow is almost nil, yet he must come across in the novel as a living and convincing person and not as an abstraction: the Professional Revolutionary. It is by giving him this speech mannerism that Malraux tries to put Katow within our reach.

Yet to say that Katow is *only* a political man of action would be to simplify things. He has a "human" side to him which is suddenly and unexpectedly revealed in a conversation with Hemmelrich who is devoured by guilt for refusing to harbour Tchen in his house:

> —J'ai connu ça, ou presque. Et aussi ton espèce de . . . rage . . . Comment veux-tu qu'on comprenne les choses autrement que par les souvenirs . . . C'est pour ça que tu ne me vexes pas.
> . . .
> —Un homme qui se fout de tout, s'il rencontre tellement le d'vouement, le sacrifice, un quelconque de ces trucs-là, il est perdu.
> —Sans blagues! Alors qu'est-ce qu'il fait?
> —Du sadisme, répondit Katow, le regardant tranquillement.
> Le grillon. Des pas, dans la rue, se perdaient peu à peu.

—Le sadisme avec les épingles, reprit-il, c'est rare; avec les paroles, c'est loin de l'être. Mais si la femme accepte 'bsolument, si elle est capable d'aller au delà . . . J'ai connu un type qui a pris et joué l'argent que la sienne avait éc'nomisé pendant des années pour aller au san'torium. Question de vie ou de mort. Il l'a perdu. (Dans ces cas-là, on perd t'jours.) Il est revenue en morceaux, 'bsolument écrasé comme toi en ce moment. Elle l'a regardé s'approcher de son lit. Elle a tout de suite compris, vois-tu. Et puis, quoi? Elle a essayé de le consoler.

The passage shows that Katow is capable of friendship, it also shows a Katow who has suffered, for it is quite clear that in the rather self-consciously Dostoievskian scene of the gambler he talks about himself although he will deny it. Later on in the same passage a further more important touch is added to this "human" side of Katow:

—Il ne faut demander aux cam'rades que ce qu'il peuvent faire. Je veux des cam'rades et pas des saints. Pas confiance dans les saints . . .
—C'est vrai, que tu as accompagné volontairement les types aux mines de plomb?
—J'étais au camp, dit Katow gêné: les mines ou le camp, ça se vaut.

The importance of this exchange lies in linking Katow's action with the idea of saintliness.

These human touches, Katow's warmth, his generosity, above all his disregard of himself are, of course, absolutely necessary for they prepare the reader for Katow's last and greatest sacrifice of which the action to accompany his comrades to the lead mines is a prefiguration. This scene with which *La Condition humaine* comes to its climax and in a way to its end is beyond doubt the finest scene in the novel. Its meaning is wholly contained in the concrete representation. There is no intrusive symbolism, nothing is explained. It is also in this scene that the taut, terse style of Malraux and especially the extraordinarily intense visual quality of his writing are used with the greatest effectiveness: nothing is described yet everything is shown and seen.

The scene takes place in the courtyard of a school when the defeated communists have been assembled waiting to be burned alive. Katow, wounded, finds himself next to Kyo (this coincidence is rather contrived) and next to two terrified Chinese one of whom, Souen, was a companion of Tchen:

Malgré la rumeur, malgré tous ces hommes qui avaient combattu comme lui, Katow était seul, seul entre le corps de son ami mort et ses deux compagnons épouvantés, seul entre ce mur et ce sifflet perdu dans la nuit. Mais un homme pouvait être plus fort que cette solitude et même, peut-être, que ce sifflet atroce: la peur luttait en lui contre la plus terrible tentation de sa vie. Il ouvrit à son tour la boucle de sa ceinture. Enfin:

—Hé là, dit-il à voix trés basse. Souen, pose ta main sur ma poitrine, et prends dès que je la toucherai: je vais vous donner mon cyanure._ Il n'y en a 'bsolument que pour deux.

. . . Les gardes masquaient la lumière, qui les entourait d'une auréole trouble; mais n'allaient-ils pas bouger? Impossible de voir quoi que ce fût; ce don de plus que sa vie, Katow le faisait à cette main chaude qui reposait sur lui, pas même à des corps, pas même à des voix.

The cyanide is lost in the darkness, then found again:

O résurrection! . . . Mais:
—Tu es sûr que ce ne sont pas des cailloux? demanda l'autre.
Il y avait beaucoup de morceaux de plâtre par terre.
—Donne! dit Katow.
Du bout des doigts, il reconnut les formes.
Il les rendit—les rendit—serra plus fort la main qui cherchait à nouveau la sienne, et attendit, tremblant des épaules, claquant des dents. 'Pourvu que le cyanure ne soit pas décomposé, malgré le papier d'argent', pensa-t-il. La main qu'il tenait tordit soudain la sienne, et, comme s'il eût communiqué par elle avec le corps perdu dans l'obscurité, il sentit que celui-ci se tendait. Il enviait cette suffocation convulsive. Presque en même temps, l'autre: un cri étranglé auquel nul ne prit garde. Puis, rien.

What we have here is the ultimate expression of what Malraux calls (perhaps out of a certain *pudeur*) *la fraternité virile* but which is, in fact, love. The greatest gift which man can give ("ce don de plus que sa vie") is his death.

Malraux's *Storm in Shanghai*

LeRoy C. Breunig

The fact that Malraux was born with the century prompts one to look back on his life in terms of decades, his twenties coinciding with *the* twenties, his sixties with the sixties, and so on. I have chosen to glance at only one of these blocks, the thirties, not only because it witnessed the publication of the novel that is usually considered his masterpiece—and I shall limit myself to that work—but also because as impressionable students, soon to become soldiers, my generation lived through the ideological battles that our immediate elders, those of Malraux's age, were waging and that were in a way crystallized in *Man's Fate*.

The *New Republic* repeated recently what has already become a cliché in France: that all of Camus and much of Sartre came out of the mold of Malraux's novels. For most readers today it is axiomatic that *La Condition humaine* is a great existentialist novel.

But that is not at all the way the thirties saw it. When the book first appeared in England in 1934, it was entitled *Storm in Shanghai*, the publishers apparently intending to sell it as a thriller, a political thriller. In the United States the Haakon Chevalier translation was called more appropriately *Man's Fate*, but almost without exception the critics ignored the implications of this title and treated it more in the spirit of the English version.

It was Edmund Wilson who discovered Malraux on this side of the Atlantic. Writing in the *New Republic* in 1933, just after the novel had originally appeared in Paris, he almost alone seems to have got the point

From *André Malraux: Metamorphosis and Imagination*, edited by Françoise Dorenlot and Micheline Tison-Braun. © 1979 by New York Literary Forum.

of the French title inspired by Montaigne. But then he goes on to conclude: "There is . . . something else in the book besides the mere theme of escape [*sic*] from the human situation. . . . His [Malraux's] interpretation of recent events seems now essentially Marxist—though he never, as I have said, slips into the facile formulas; and though the criticism his characters make of the line of the Comintern is more or less that of Trotsky, he maintains in relation to Trosky, too, an attitude of independence. Marxism, Gisors observes, is not a doctrine but a will; and it is simply that, in Malraux's world, the only men he respects are animated by the Marxist will." For Wilson there was no doubt about it; Malraux was a Marxist.

When in June 1934 the translation appeared in New York, most of the reviews were, like Wilson's, variations of the Marxist criterion. In a front page article in the *Saturday Review of Literature,* Pearl Buck, whose *Good Earth* had appeared three years before, does not let us forget that, unlike the rather frivolous French adventurer whose work she is presenting, *she* really knows China. Malraux, she writes, was "caught up by the fascination, rather than by a profound belief in the cause of the Chinese people. . . . One is confirmed . . . after reading the book that the real revolution which China is yet to have cannot come out of such figures as these, or at least out of such incomplete followers of the great Marx, however satisfactory many Marxians will certainly find this book. Rather the true revolution will come, not thus frantic and superficial but deep and basic out of the real Chinese people."

Writing in the *Nation,* Lionel Abel sees in *Man's Fate* a successful proletarian novel. According to the Marxists, he says, D. H. Lawrence, Proust, Mann, and Joyce all attest to the decay of the bourgeois world. "The bourgeois values are no longer creative, they say, and the corollary is that art and individuality are being recreated by the proletariat." *Man's Fate* supports this Marxist view. "The Shanghai insurrectionists . . . united against a common enemy as brothers in arms, hold on to their personal styles of dignity even though unable to communicate them except to themselves."

One senses some wishful thinking in this article. Abel seems to be persuading himself that one can be simultaneously a revolutionary and an individual. And we are reminded of the urgency of this question in the thirties when the phrase "come the revolution" had the ring of reality.

Abel's remarks about the decadent bourgeoisie are echoed in—of all places—the *New York Times Sunday Book Review* in order to reach a very different conclusion. R. L. Duffus claims somewhat smirkingly that although it will be the bourgeoisie that reads it—for only the bourgeoisie can afford the $2.50 that the novel costs—it will undoubtedly be received as good proletarian literature. It *must* be, because Leon Trotsky endorses it. Duffus then condemns the naive optimism of the translator, Haakon Chevalier, who in his preface alludes to the heroes of the novel and their bond of brotherhood "in pursuit of a goal to which the future of humanity is intimately linked." "Nonsense," says Duffus. This is a novel of decadent pessimism. It is not a proletarian novel at all, but the story of a thoroughly bourgeois reaction. The unhealthy qualities in the book are the product of a bourgeois disintegration. "They are the result of just such a divigation *[sic]* as in Flaubert produced *Salammbo*. They may not interfere with the book's popularity—they may even add to the sales. But they do reveal an uncertainty of purpose, a philosophical as well as a literary weakness that makes M. Malraux with all his gifts no more than a good second-rate."

And what said the *Partisan Review*, the prestigious "journal of the anti-Stalinist left-wing, cultural avant garde," which struck with awe the young Trotskyists of the CCNY Alcove 1 in the mid-thirties, according to a recent account by Irving Kristol? The *Partisan Review* ignored Malraux until 1938, when F. W. Dupee described his shifting relations with the revolutionary movement, accusing him in effect of opportunism and hypocrisy. Professor Dupee quotes a remark from *Man's Fate* uttered by Kyo to the Comintern representative: "In Marxism there is the sense of a fatality and also the exultation of a will. Every time fatality comes before will I am suspicious." And Professor Dupee goes on to accuse Malraux of oscillating between Trotsky and Stalin and of ascribing each shift to the recurrence of the "will." For example, "once the Comintern, confronted by Hitler in power, reverted to the old policy and proclaimed the people's front, it seems to have recaptured its title to the Marxist will; and Malraux once more reversed his sympathies. Trotsky now became 'a moment in the past' and those who continued to uphold revolutionary principles became so many utopian moralists."

Almost without exception, then, the reaction in America to *Man's Fate* was political. The reason is not far to seek: in that decade which went from the Crash to the Blitz we *were* political. Writing in the *New Republic* in 1938 on *Man's Hope*, the novel inspired by the Spanish civil war, Ralph Bates placed Malraux among the "progressive forces of the world." We of the thirties were progressive because we still believed in progress, in the perfectability of man. We were concerned, intellectually as well as pragmatically, with the ways and means, political, economic, social, of enhancing the well-being of mankind. As the thirties unfolded, fascism and our opposition to it merely served to strengthen our kinship with what we thought to be Malraux's revolutionary optimism. I recall my enthusiasm as a graduate student sitting one evening in the periodical room of the Cornell Library reading Haakon Chevalier's "Return of the Hero" in the *Kenyon Review:* "Malraux has brought the hero back into the novel. If as seems likely, faith in man's capacity to control his social destiny increases and the bonds of human fellowship are strengthened it may well be that Malraux's novels herald the beginning of a new heroic literature."

"The bonds of human fellowship," writes Chevalier. One can almost hear the strains of "Avanti Popolo" and the "Groupons-nous et demain" of the Internationale.

That was 1940. Only a few years later in one of the first postwar essays on Malraux, Claude-Edmonde Magny was to write: "Malraux . . . has reiterated only one point under the most diverse forms: the absolute impossibility for any individual to communicate with any other, even with those who belong to the same group." It was, of course, the watershed of World War II that separated Magny from Chevalier. This war, which caused so many literary names to topple, those whom we had studied so assiduously in our Marcel Braunschvig anthology, *La Littérature française contemporaine,* in the mid-thirties: Barbusse, Dorgelès, Rolland, Romains (not to mention the conservatives Bordeaux, Bourget, Estaunié, even Daudet and Loti)— this war brought Malraux into his own at a time when Pascal and Kierkegaard were tending to crowd out the names of Stalin and Trotsky in literary criticism.

Malraux himself helped in the postwar evaluation of his novel. An anthology that was to replace Braunschvig for the students of the fifties, Gaëtan Picon's *Panorama de la nouvelle littérature française,* included (in French, of course) the following quotation from Malraux's *La Psychologie de l'art:* "A few years ago I told the story of a man who does not recognize his voice that has just been recorded because he hears it for the first time through his ear and no longer through his throat; and because our throat alone transmits our inner voice I called the book *La Condition humaine.*" It is hard to imagine a more graphic illustration of Sartre's notion of the "Other."

A new adjective, *tragic,* creeps into the commentaries on *Man's Fate* after the war. We find it used by two of the American pioneers of the new focus on Malraux: W. M. Frohock, at the time an assistant professor at Columbia, whose *André Malraux and the Tragic Imagination* was to appear in 1952, and Bert Leefmans, a graduate student of Professor Frohock, whose "Malraux and Tragedy: the structure of *La Condition humaine*" came out in the *Romanic Review* in 1953.

Actually, the word *tragic* was not completely new, and it seems appropriate to end this little glance at the thirties with a tribute to the one American critic I could find who, when *Man's Fate* first appeared in 1934, came closest to seeing it for what it was to become. The French writer Ernest Hello once said of the true critic that he "must be as accurate as posterity; he must speak in the present the words of the future." John Chamberlain of the daily *New York Times* was just such a critic when he wrote: "Malraux may lack the marvelous invention of incident that one finds in Dostoevsky, he may lack the cosmic brooding of Joseph Conrad, but he has nevertheless something in common with these writers; he too sees into the mire. The perception of this as 'man's fate' is what endows his writing with the tragic sense of life."

André Malraux: The Commitment to Action in *La Condition humaine*

Derek W. Allan

In an excellent article published in 1948, which deserves closer attention than it has so far received, Nicola Chiaromonte writes that:

> André Malraux has pushed to its extreme consequences that modern pragmatic impulse which tends to see in the world of action the only reality, and, what is more, to reject any proposition which cannot be translated into a force, an act or a series of acts.

The present article seeks to examine some of the implications of this assessment as they apply to Malraux's third, and perhaps most influential, novel, *La Condition humaine*. It will be argued here that the perspective offered by Chiaromonte's statement goes to the very heart of the world view embodied in this novel and in particular that it is of key importance to an accurate understanding of the novel's central character, the revolutionary leader, Kyo Gisors. The underlying, controlling principle of *La Condition humaine,* it will be contended, stems precisely from a "pragmatic impulse"—a tendency to regard action, with its concomitant world of practical, tangible consequences, as the sole reliable source of meaning. The impulse is one which Chiaromonte quite properly terms "modern," since it constitutes a highly characteristic expression of the prevailing twentieth-century mood which so frequently displays a deep distrust of abstractions of any kind, and which consents to rest its faith only in what can be seen and touched, here and now—the concrete, "observable" fact.

From *French Forum* 6, no. 1 (January 1981). © 1981 by French Forum Publishers, Inc.

Critics of *La Condition humaine* have seldom failed to comment on the importance of action, particularly where the character of Kyo is concerned. However, with the exception of Nicola Chiaromonte, the prevalent critical tendency has been to conclude that the fundamental dimension of the novel lies elsewhere and that the function of action should ultimately be assigned a secondary importance only. Many critics, for example, have contended that each of the major characters is primarily intent on seeking some form of escape—or perhaps a kind of Pascalian "divertissement"—from a human condition which very broadly speaking is described as that state of oppressive meaninglessness and alienation which results from the complete collapse of all credible value systems. Together with other alternatives such as eroticism, mythomania, and the will to power, action is said to offer a possible means of escape from this predicament, or a possible means through which the human condition may, in the terminology of certain critics, be "transcended." Viewed in this light, action itself is clearly not the issue of central concern. Action is merely one among several alternatives which might be adopted in order to pursue the ultimate objective, which is the attempt to escape from or "transcend" the human condition.

The interpretation of *La Condition humaine* offered in the present article involves a major revision of these aspects of prevailing critical opinion. Contrary to the frequent practice of assigning action a secondary or dependent role, the analysis which follows places action squarely at the prime focus of attention and sees it, unequivocally, as the fundamental value of the novel. In the present instance, *La Condition humaine* will be approached principally through two of the main characters, Kyo Gisors and the "baron" de Clappique, but an analysis of these two characters ultimately illustrates the more general point that Malraux's underlying intention throughout this novel is to explore the characteristics of a world portrayed solely in terms of the potentialities and limitations of practical, clear-sighted action. In Chiaromonte's words, Malraux confronts us here with a world in which action is "the only reality"—a world which "rejects any proposition which cannot be translated into a force, an act, or a series of acts." Far from playing a role of secondary importance, action in this context forms the very mould in which all experience of the world is cast.

In addition to this, the present article takes issue with the widespread critical tendency to stress the notions of divertissement, or escape, to explain the function of action in *La Condition humaine*. Such interpretations, which depict action as one possible form of distraction or release from an oppressive and "absurd" reality, are undoubtedly influenced to some degree by the example of Pascal. They are perhaps also modeled, even if unconsciously, on the stereotyped image of the soldier of fortune (the French Foreign Legionnaire perhaps?) who plunges headlong into some difficult and dangerous enterprise in order to blot out the painful memories of a world he has left behind. Fundamentally, action in a context such as this is intended as an antidote to lucidity. The crucial point to be grasped in *La Condition humaine,* however, is that far from serving as a means of avoiding unpalatable truths and escaping from reality, action in this novel affirms its characteristic twentieth-century function and constitutes the means by which reality is *defined.* Action becomes the fountainhead of all reliable knowledge about the real world: it constitutes the very source of all meaning and the principle upon which all truth—palatable or unpalatable—is founded.

How, then, does this principle operate, and what kind of "definition of reality" does it produce?

It is important to stress, first of all, what is *not* at issue here. One is not, as some critics appear to be, in search of some form of ethical system founded on action—as if action could somehow serve as a basis for universally applicable, ready-made formulae designed to distinguish good from evil in human affairs. Still less, as other critics seem to imply, is it a question of demonstrating that action is in some way a principle superior to others that might be opposed to it, such as contemplation or introspection, for example. The question at stake relates rather to a fundamental issue of perception and comprehension. One is asking: What kind of world does action body forth when it becomes the sole source and determinant of reality? What would a world be like in which the original, bewildering chaos of things and events is given order and significance—its *only* order and significance—through the potentialities and limitations of that most ordinary of human experiences, practical action?

One can begin to discern the outlines of this highly pragmatic attitude in the following, very characteristic passage, which occurs early in part 1 of *La Condition humaine.* At this point in the novel, the revolutionary leader, Kyo Gisors, is considering the state of preparedness of his forces just prior to the uprising in Shanghai. Organizational duties take Kyo to the city's squalid, poverty-stricken districts from which the revolutionary forces are to draw their major support. As he walks through these areas, teeming with human misery and degradation, his attitude towards them—and, by implication, towards the revolution—emerges clearly:

> "Un bon quartier," pensa Kyo. Depuis plus d'un mois que, de comité en comité, il préparait l'insurrection, il avait cessé de voir

les rues: il ne marchait plus dans la boue, mais sur un plan. Le
grattement des millions de petites vies quotidiennes disparaissait,
écrasé par une autre vie. Les concessions, les quartiers riches,
avec leurs grilles lavées par la pluie à l'extrémité des rues, n'ex-
istaient plus que comme des menaces, des barrières, de longs
murs de prison sans fenêtres; ces quartiers atroces, au contraire—
ceux où les troupes de choc étaient les plus nombreuses—, pal-
pitaient du frémissement d'une multitude à l'affût. Au tournant
d'une ruelle, son regard tout à coup s'engouffra dans la profondeur des lumières d'une large rue; bien que voilée par la pluie
battante, elle conservait dans son esprit sa perspective, car il
faudrait l'attaquer contre des fusils, des mitrailleuses, qui tireraient de toute sa profondeur.

This passage merits close and careful consideration. It is important to
note that the spectacle of these "quartiers atroces" does not prompt Kyo
to any of the conventional expressions of pity or indignation; nor (despite
what many critics have suggested to the contrary) does it urge him to seek
explanations for this mass suffering through the categories of any social or
economic theory. Instead, his reactions are purely pragmatic: he views the
situation solely through the eyes of a tactician, thinking only of the practical
implications of what he sees and the part these factors will play in the
immediate future of the uprising. The area through which he is walking is
the one in which the revolutionary "shock troops" are the most numerous
and, therefore, despite its extreme poverty and degradation, it is, for him,
"un bon quartier." The miserable daily struggle for existence of the poor
yields place in his consciousness to the role these men and women are to
play in the coming events: he thinks only of their place in the plan of action.
His attitude towards the wealthy areas, the areas occupied by the ruling
elite, follows the same pattern. The rich are not seen as the incarnation of
some general historical force: they are not "the capitalists," or "the stan-
dard-bearers of private property," or the "exploiting classes." For Kyo,
the significance of these "quartiers riches" derives solely from their immediate, practical importance: here, the revolutionary shock troops will
meet resistance and counterattack. The wealthy areas are, therefore, seen
simply as obstacles or threats: "des menaces, des barrières, de longs murs
de prison sans fenêtres." Finally, even the very street into which Kyo turns
is perceived solely in terms of its practical significance: he visualizes it
clearly, despite the driving rain, "car il faudrait l'attaquer contre des fusils,
des mitrailleuses, qui tireraient de toute sa profondeur."

Right throughout *La Condition humaine,* Kyo's experience of the Shanghai uprising is consistently presented in this way. At no time does he attempt to explain this vast collective event in terms of any social or economic theory; at no time does this event appear to him as the gradual, inevitable unfolding of historical forces; in short, at no time does he have recourse to any abstraction—to any *idea.* His grasp on revolutionary events is established and maintained solely through his appreciation of the tangible implications of *action currently taking place.* He is the total pragmatist who, in Chiaromonte's words, has decided to "reject any proposition which cannot be translated directly into a force, an act, or a series of acts."

There is no suggestion at any point throughout *La Condition humaine* that this reliance on action necessarily implies a desire for violence. The subject of violence has attracted many of Malraux's critics, and there is obviously good reason for this. Where Kyo is concerned, however, it is essential to recognize that, although the exigencies of particular situations may at times demand a violent response, violence is in no sense an intrinsic or indispensable part of his experience of action. To misunderstand this is to miss the basic point at issue: Kyo perceives the changing world of events through the eyes of the determined pragmatist who, once having espoused a cause of action, bends all his energies to the daily task of ensuring its continued success. If such a cause is one that involves a mass uprising—as Kyo's is—violence may well be a necessary instrument when circumstances require it. But violence for its own sake—violence when there is no practical need for it—is quite outside this frame of reference and quite foreign to Kyo's character. At best, such conduct would be pointless; at worst, when tactically foolish, it might well constitute a recipe for disaster. Any such a priori bias towards violence must, sooner or later, offend against the basic canon of the pragmatist's creed, which requires that action should be adapted to circumstances—that action should prove *effective.*

It is worthwhile noting that this emphasis on the need for effectiveness in action throws light on the motivation for Kyo's adherence to the Communist Party. This issue has always proved a major stumbling block to critics, since they have been faced with Malraux's own unequivocal statements made on many occasions throughout his life, that Marxism as a theory of history held little interest for him. Kyo, however, like Malraux himself, sees something else in Marxism besides the claim to have unveiled the mysteries of historical processes. Kyo sees what might be described as the Leninist dimension of Marxism—the determination, and the capacity, to create and maintain a viable and effective mass political movement. It is not the ideology of Marxism that appeals to Kyo: it is the Communist

Party itself, which offers him the means of acting, and acting effectively, within the context of a large collective enterprise. In this respect, Kyo is indistinguishable from Garine, the central character of Malraux's first novel, *Les Conquérants*. Garine is attracted to the Bolsheviks because "Il comprit vite qu'il avait affaire . . . non à des prédicateurs mais à des techniciens." And like Kyo, Garine has a dual attitude towards these "technicians" of revolution: "Si la technique et le goût de l'insurrection, chez les bolcheviks, le séduisaient, le vocabulaire doctrinal et surtout le dogmatisme qui les chargaient l'exaspéraient." Marxism as the inspiration and vehicle for collective action is seen as an admirable creation, but Marxism as a body of doctrine claiming to represent "scientific socialism" is merely a pointless exercise in mystification. Kyo himself sums up this attitude succinctly in the course of a disagreement with the doctrinaire Communist leader, Vologuine, at a crucial stage of the Shanghai uprising: "Il y a dans le marxisme le sens d'une fatalité, et l'exultation d'une volonté. Chaque fois que la fatalité passe avant la volonté, je me méfie."

It should be emphasized, of course, that this indifference—occasionally open hostility—towards what Garine terms "doctrinal trash" is not confined to Marxism alone. Kyo and Garine are equally unmoved by all other social, economic, or even psychological theories that lay claim to some element of permanence or generality. Both characters, as representatives of a typically twentieth-century state of mind, have simply resolved to abandon all sources of meaning that make appeal to any form of the "eternal," no matter how residual. Instead, they rely entirely on the series of transient and particular truths that are revealed in and through the concrete *act* itself. They embody an attitude which Albert Camus has described admirably in *Le Mythe de Sisyphe* in his characterization of "le conquérant," a figure who bears a striking resemblance to certain of Malraux's heroes, and to Kyo in particular: "Je n'ai rien à faire des idées ou de l'éternel," explains "le conquérant": "Les vérités qui sont à ma mesure, la main peut les toucher. Je ne puis me séparer d'elles. Voilà pourquoi vous ne pouvez rien fonder sur moi: rien ne dure du conquérant."

Camus's description is a penetrating one not only because it points to the strength of this pragmatic attitude—the fact that it does provide a source of truth—but also because it suggests the existence of limitations which the man of action must accept. Malraux himself is keenly aware that there are such limitations, and while Kyo and Garine illustrate the strength and lucidity that may be drawn from action, much of Malraux's attention in his early novels is devoted to an exploration of the serious restrictions which this reliance on action also implies. Not that there is any suggestion that action thereby stands condemned as a viable source of truth. To delimit the area within which a value may successfully operate is not to condemn it as invalid: it is merely to describe it the more accurately and to recognize its proper character. Malraux is determined to confront the limitations of action without compromise, with the result that the universe of *La Condition humaine,* for example, emerges as one in which truth is certainly *possible*— but possible only if one is prepared to accept certain conditions, and the sometimes tragic consequences which these conditions imply.

The operation of these principles is well illustrated by the circumstances that lead up to Kyo's arrest and eventual execution at the hands of the Kuomintang. Not long before his arrest, Kyo is warned by the "baron" de Clappique that his life is now in imminent danger. Clappique himself has been given just one day to flee Shanghai, and his contact in the Kuomintang hierarchy has made it clear that Kyo's life is now also in jeopardy. Kyo interprets this information—correctly—as confirmation that the Kuomintang have joined forces with the Western powers and are preparing to attack their former allies, the Communists. He is under no illusions and, particularly since his discussions with Vologuine in Hankow, fully realizes that these developments pose grave threats for the Communists, whose military position now appears very vulnerable. Clappique's advice to Kyo in this situation is quite simple: abandon the Communist forces to their dangerous predicament, go into hiding, and flee the city within forty-eight hours. The alternative for Kyo is to remain and organize the Communist defense, running the risk of capture and execution. Clappique himself is attempting to arrange his own escape immediately.

This is clearly a critical moment for Kyo, and one which Malraux is at pains to highlight for the obvious importance it bears. How should Kyo react to this situation? Should he follow Clappique's advice and simply abandon his fellow Communists, or should he remain and continue to play his part in the perilous struggle at hand? Most importantly, what significance do these alternatives have for him? Would the decision to remain represent little more than a meaningless display of barren heroics? Or, alternatively, would there be good reason for such a course of action, and is it possible that a decision to flee would constitute an abject capitulation, implying perhaps a definitive abandonment of the pursuit of meaning and genuine identity?

Strangely enough, critics of *La Condition humaine* have rarely paid serious attention to this crucial moment in Kyo's experience. Much has been written, of course, about Kyo's heroism in general and his courage in defense of the cause he has espoused. But almost invariably, attention has been focused on the fortitude he displays *after his arrest* by the Kuomintang, particularly as he awaits execution. Now, while these closing scenes are obviously highly relevant to the question of Kyo's heroism, they do, nonetheless, depict a character who is no longer a free agent capable of saving his life if he wishes. In these final hours, Kyo has become a captive doomed to be executed, without the slightest hope of escape. His situation has changed drastically since the previous day, when Clappique gave him advance warning of the Kuomintang threat and counseled immediate flight. At this earlier stage, Kyo is master of his own fate, and nothing prevents him from making good his escape and guaranteeing his own safety if he so wishes. His decision at this point to remain in Shanghai is, therefore, a momentous one, and it is this decision that merits our primary attention if the full force of his character, and the nature of his reliance on action, are to be properly understood.

Why, then, does he remain?

One critic who has fully recognized the need to understand Kyo's decision at this crucial moment is Nicola Chiaromonte; and in seeking to explain the grounds for Kyo's decision, one could scarcely do better than refer to what Chiaromonte has written: "The first thing to be said," this critic points out,

> is that neither Malraux nor his characters accept for a moment the idea that one can withdraw from an action in which one has chosen to be involved. By withdrawing, one would become a comedian, renouncing the very substance of identity, which requires acceptance of the fact that life is essentially tragic, not a game whose rules the individual can change at will.

In other words, if an action is abandoned *because* it is leading to grave consequences—which would have been precisely Kyo's attitude if he had chosen to flee Shanghai—the implication is that the only acceptable kind of action is action that will not produce such results: action could rightfully claim one's commitment only if a guarantee was included that it *would never lead to undesirable consequences* (such as the Kuomintang attack, for example).

To ask for such a guarantee, however, is clearly to impose an *unreal* condition—a condition which flies in the face of the simple evidence of common sense. It implies that the consequences of action are controllable, that nothing can ever result which is not desired. To adopt Chiaromonte's words, it implies that "life . . . is a game whose rules the individual can change at will." Kyo is able to rely on action as his source of knowledge about the *real* world only because he accepts the condition that the real world imposes—the possibility that an action may lead to unintended and undesirable consequences. His decision to remain in Shanghai is, accordingly, the price he pays for his continuing grasp on the world of real events and for preserving what Chiaromonte aptly terms his "identity"—his awareness of the part he plays in those events. To abandon the Communist forces at this point would be to lose this grasp on reality and enter a world of pretense—an impossible world in which revolutions never founder and where the possibility of a tragic conclusion is ruled out *ab initio*. His refusal to take this option is a measure of the extent to which he values his lucid awareness of meaning in things and events: the clear, unequivocal implication is that he values this highly enough to risk death rather than lose it—an attitude that can rightly be termed heroic.

This crucial point has been overlooked by virtually all of Malraux's critics, and it warrants further emphasis. Kyo, we do well to remember, can have recourse to no other source of meaning outside action. He cannot, for example, appeal to the categories of historical theory and confer meaning on a possible Communist defeat as (for instance) a "necessary phase in the development of the socialist Revolution." Kyo's sole source of meaning is action: either he understands revolutionary events through action, or he does not understand them at all. Accordingly, it is the logic of action that he must rely on, even in the extreme situation posed by the threat of imminent defeat. And the logic of action is as clear as it is implacable: to desert a cause once espoused is to exchange the plenitude of meaning for the emptiness of pretense—the real for the unreal. It would be quite incorrect, therefore, to imagine that Kyo's decision to remain in Shanghai results from some arbitrary and unexplained notion of revolutionary loyalty, or from some rash, ill-considered impulse. Kyo stays in Shanghai because his value—the principle that gives meaning to his life—*demands* that he stay, or else abandon all hope of meaning. In a sense he has no choice: action will not permit the option of flight, since to flee is to refuse to comply with the terms upon which it is capable of granting meaning to things and events. For, to reiterate: the decision to flee implies, quite unequivocally, that the consequences of action are controllable, and this proposition is in flagrant contradiction with the simple evidence of everyday human experience and elementary common sense. A world modeled on the terms of such a proposition may certainly be conceivable, but it would be nothing more than a world of pure fantasy, a land of inconsequential make-believe, far removed from the real world in which revolutionary events (for example) have their being.

Malraux takes great pains to drive this point home, and, not content with exploring the issue solely through the character of Kyo, he goes on to ask: What would a character be like whose commitment to action was always accompanied by the *determination to withdraw* at the first sign that undesirable consequences were likely to result? This question, which implies an attitude towards action exactly the reverse of Kyo's, is fully answered in the character of Clappique. For the refusal to accept all the consequences of action is, in fact, the very basis upon which the structure of Clappique's character is founded, and it is for precisely this reason that he appears consistently as the compulsive buffoon, or the "comedian," to borrow Chiaromonte's apt term. Clappique turns his back on the possibility of serious commitment to any action and, since he is thereby deprived of the possibility of any real identity, he is forced to rely on a series of comic masks: "comic" because none of his actions must ever lead to serious consequences; "masks" because any identity which action may fleetingly lend him must be able to be produced and discarded at will.

Expressed at the level of ordinary day-to-day contact with others, Clappique's attitude manifests itself in a blend of unrelieved whimsicality and vapid make-believe. None of his moods or emotions ever genuinely involves him; he adopts them and casts them aside quite arbitrarily. If, on occasion, he does desire something more closely resembling a distinctive and consistent personality, he appeals to a prefabricated model borrowed from the world of fiction, his choice quite naturally falling on that branch of fiction in which the very shape and form of reality can be changed at will—the realm of fantasy. Hence, his recurrent imitations of Fantômas and Punch (and, one might add, his special affection for the *Arabian Nights* and the *Tales of Hoffmann*). None of this, however, is capable of producing what Chiaromonte aptly terms the "substance of identity" and, as Clappique himself confesses, in a characteristically theatrical manner, "Le baron de Clappique n'existe pas."

Critics have interpreted the character of Clappique in a variety of ways, but common to all these interpretations has been a tendency to focus on the more readily discernible features of this character without pointing to any firm, underlying principle from which these features may clearly be seen to originate. Denis Boak, for example, writes that "[Clappique] wishes to escape from himself by actually becoming someone else." This evidently refers to Clappique's continual adoption and rejection of a series of artificial roles. But Boak does not supply a sufficient reason for this behavior. He describes it as "an attempt at self-transcendence," but this carries the issue little further, since, in Boak's view, *all* the major characters of *La Condition humaine* are engaged in "the creation of . . . a set of transcendental values."

The basis of Clappique's particular form of "transcendence" is not made clear. In a somewhat similar vein, the critic Joseph Hoffmann has described Clappique as "un homme qui vit dans le mensonge, . . . un être qui vit tout entier en dehors de lui-même, qui essaie de sortir de sa condition d'homme en s'échappant à soi-même, en se réfugiant dans le mensonge et la bouffonnerie." Yet Hoffmann regards this attempt to "sortir de la condition d'homme" as common to all the major characters of *La Condition humaine*. Why, then, does Clappique's means of "escape" take this particular form? By what *process* has he become "un homme qui vit dans le mensonge"? The issue is far less to know that Clappique distorts and falsifies reality (that much is quite clear) than to know precisely why this is so. The reason for this—the reason for his role-playing and for his need to take refuge in "le mensonge"—is that his refusal to become unreservedly involved in action—in any action—necessarily implies a definitive and irreparable breach with the real world. For, to repeat, action can establish and maintain a grasp on reality only for one (such as Kyo) who, having recognized that the consequences of action are controllable only in a world of fantasy, determines not to relinquish the cause he has espoused, wherever it may lead. Clappique's endless comic masquerade is the direct expression of the radical loss of contact with the real world which results from the refusal to accept any such genuinely serious commitment. The fundamental reason for Clappique's need to take refuge in "le mensonge" is, quite simply, that he refuses to accept the only possible terms under which action may serve as a source of truth.

It is not the intention of the present discussion to proceed to a more detailed study of the character of Clappique. The issue has been introduced at this point simply to underline the importance which attaches to this question of withdrawal from action in *La Condition humaine* and to contrast Clappique's attitude with that of Kyo. Sufficient has perhaps been said of Clappique, however, to indicate that the attitude towards action which he embodies constitutes an attempt to lay claim to a power which is, quite literally, the attribute of a *god*. For, by refusing to accept all the consequences of action, and in claiming a right of veto over any decree of fate which he regards as unduly inauspicious, he is seeking to assume the quality of *omnipotence*—the completely unfettered power to alter the shape of reality to suit his wishes. Clappique would consent to wholehearted commitment to a course of action only in a world in which he also controlled all the strings of fate which might determine the final outcome. He would act with resolve, as Kyo does, only in a blissful, submissive world in which the course of events would infallibly adapt itself to suit his desires—a world in which the virtue of resolution would, by definition, be superfluous. Such is the nature of Clappique's strange, impossible ambition. He seeks to be not just powerful, but all-powerful—not man, but god.

This "volonté de déité," as Kyo's father terms it (expressly applying the phrase to Clappique), is the temptation which Kyo is able to resist in his decision to remain in Shanghai despite the imminent Kuomintang attack. At this crucial turning point in the novel, Kyo rejects the pretense of omnipotence and accepts the limitation which a world of human dimensions imposes—the possibility that the fortunes of an action may lead to undesirable (and, in this case, fatal) consequences. In this way, Kyo retains his grasp on the world of human experience. He resists "la volonté de déité" and opts to remain a man, among other men, despite the heavy price which may need to be paid. In other words, Kyo accepts the "condition" which action imposes if the perspective it grants is to remain "human"—he accepts (just as Clappique refuses to accept) the "human condition."

This final point—Kyo's capacity to *accept* the human condition—has been the subject of considerable misunderstanding by Malraux's critics. As mentioned earlier in this article, it has very frequently been argued that all the characters of *La Condition humaine,* including Kyo, are intent on seeking relief from the human condition and *escaping* from it if possible. Cecil Jenkins, for example, depicts the human condition as the experience of "a dark and airless world . . . a world where all men are victims, where all are constantly living their death," and this critic goes on to contend that all the characters are seeking some form of Pascalian divertissement from this grim predicament. Similarly, Denis Boak describes the human condition as a state of meaningless futility and maintains that "Each one [of the characters] is seeking to escape from the human condition by the creation of his own set of transcendental values."

Yet, however useful such interpretations may be in other contexts, they are quite inappropriate and misleading when applied to *La Condition humaine.* Far from implying that the escape from the human condition is a desirable goal, Malraux's novel depicts the option of escape as leading to an extreme deterioration in the quality of human experience, while, on the contrary, the highest possible value is placed on the capacity to *accept* the human condition. For, as we have seen, Malraux's concept of the human condition has a clear and specific meaning which is quite unlike the interpretations of Jenkins and Boak referred to above. Central to Malraux's concept is the idea of a necessary human limitation—a requirement which must be fulfilled if life is to retain those qualities which mark it out as something of value. In essence, the human condition, as Malraux portrays it, is the limitation, or "condition," imposed by action which must be observed if the world revealed through action is to retain its "human" features. It is the condition which, if transgressed, leads directly to the *in*human. As the analysis above has shown, Clappique seeks to escape from this condition through his refusal to renounce the right to withdraw from action, and the consequence is his inhuman pretense of omnipotence—his pitiable capitulation to "la volonté de déité" and his state of permanent exile to a world of empty fantasy. Kyo, however, accepts the condition which action imposes: he relinquishes the right to withdraw, and the consequence of this is that he remains firmly anchored in the world of human experience—the concrete, tangible world of real revolutionary events—and is able to know, even moments before his death, that he is dying "pour avoir donné un sens à sa vie." Far from representing an ideal objective, the attempt to escape from the human condition is, in the final analysis, an abandonment of human life and its possibilities of meaning. The willingness to accept the human condition signifies a determination to realize those possibilities, however costly that course of action may be.

Gisors and the Human Condition

W. M. Frohock

Few passages in Malraux's novels have been so thoroughly worked over by his exegetes as the one in *La Condition humaine* in which the old intellectual Gisors tries to explain to the industrialist-financier Ferral what it means to be a man. Until the publication of *Les Voix du silence* in 1951 critics had no choice but to take this statement as Malraux's final word on the subject. Not as Gisors's final word, which it was, but as Malraux's, which it manifestly was not. They wrote so much about it that the present attempt to revive something quite so threadbare may seem superfluous, and perhaps presumptuous as well.

My excuse is that, perforce, the early commentators could not read the Gisors-Ferral remarks in the light of Malraux's subsequent writings; they did not have this changed illumination to reveal the way we should read the passage and the relative importance we should attach to the reading we obtain. Now that we have the entire canon and have heard Malraux as he "speaks in his own voice," particularly in the essays on art, we should be able to see just how awkward the subject was for an author working under the restraints and obligations that devolve on any novelist. And we should cease to treat what Gisors says as anything but a first tentative statement, which Malraux would spend much of his later life refining.

The psychological implausibility of the Gisors-Ferral episode seems to have disturbed few early readers. Now it strikes one immediately. This old man has been presented as a model of almost catatonic calm. He has helped

From *Mélanges Malraux Miscellany* 14, no. 2 (Autumn 1982). © 1982 by Walter G. Langlois.

instigate a revolution but is too inert to take an active part in it. His son is one of the leaders, and he loves his son dearly. He has had a telephone call telling him that Kyo is safe, but he is still so disturbed that he has come out into the streets in search of confirmation. Yet he willingly postpones his quest for news to share a café table with an individual whom he not only suspects of being an unredeemed liar and thus a bad source of news, but also knows to be actively committed to frustrating and throttling the revolution. True, the anonymous narrator explains that since Kyo's revolutionary role is unknown to the public Gisors can afford to be seen with Ferral, but he offers not the shadow of a reason why he should tolerate company that could only be odious to him. And that he should initiate a metaphysical colloquy in these circumstances, and with such a repugnant partner, is surely no less difficult to believe.

Furthermore, the usefulness of the scene in the general economy of the novel is dubious. It hardly can be said to advance the narrative since no later event grows out of it. It reveals nothing we do not already know about Ferral's character: the episode follows directly upon the one in which he releases the entire stock of a pet shop in Valérie Serge's hotel room, so that the reader is quite aware that the tycoon is vindictive, intent on dominating people around him, and excessively upset when his will is frustrated. In addition, what we take the scene to show about Gisors's inconstancy of purpose may not be at all what Malraux intended.

Is the scene in the right place? A reader who can detect no compelling necessity for its appearing in the novel at this point rather than at any of a number of others may suspect that the novelist wrote the scene first and later had to decide where to insert it in his text. We know that Malraux was hesitant at times about keeping or dropping whole passages he had written for one novel or another. The late Professor of the History of Science at M.I.T., Giorgio de Santillana, who was with him in Spain, used to tell how Malraux would come to a café of an evening with a sheaf of freshly written pages, read them to friends at his table and discuss where they would best fit in L'Espoir. The character of the whimsical archeologist, Rensky, appears, disappears, and reappears in various editions of Les Conquérants. A prose portrait of Borodin, written for the same novel, was pulled apart and the parts distributed piecemeal through the volume. A long section of the account of Baron Clappique's last night in Shanghai was excised from La Condition humaine before the novel went to press. Whole sentences and even paragraphs were moved from one place to another in Le Temps du mépris between the serial publication and the publication in book form. Such instances suggest that Malraux was not the kind of writer who, like

Flaubert, knows where every scrap of prose will go before he writes it. But of course one can only surmise: I know of nothing to prove conclusively that the episode here in question occurs where it does as the result of a post facto choice.

However this may be, critics were sorely tempted to lift the episode out of context and discuss Gisors's ideas as if they were Malraux's own. In later years he would complain about the irresponsibility of readers of his novels who attributed the ideas of his characters to himself, but in this instance one sympathizes with those who yielded to the temptation. It is so easy to forget that the scene is part of a fiction that the sin seems venial. We stand to gain in comprehension, however, by insisting on putting Gisors back into the novel, so to speak.

His social and intellectual behavior seem somewhat compulsive. It is Gisors who introduces the matter of the human condition and in fact forces it upon Ferral. The latter has just asked him whether willingness to die for an idea is not typical of human stupidity, and his abrupt reply is so oblique as almost to amount to a non-sequitur: "Il est rare qu'un homme puisse supporter—comment dirai-je?—sa condition d'homme." It is Gisors who insists on returning to the subject when Ferral's conversation shifts to an affirmation that a man is what he does—the sum of his acts. And it is also he who, as the scene continues and Ferral becomes less and less interested, does more and more of the talking, until finally what began as dialogue tends to become a simple monologue.

Like Garcia in *L'Espoir* and Vincent Berger in *Les Noyers de l'Altenburg,* Gisors is one of those older men whom Malraux endows with special insight into the characters of those around them. Over the years he has developed a kind of empathy that allows him to understand other individuals by recognizing in them one aspect or another of his own character. He has perceived in Ferral something like the Nietzschean will to power. Although the subject seems at first as broadly inclusive as humanity itself, Gisors immediately restricts it by framing his definition in terms of Ferral's dominant trait, offering him an analysis of the human situation that, given his particular character, should mean the most to him. Nothing authorizes us to assume that he would propose the same formulae to the terrorist Tchen, the *farfelu* Clappique, or Kyo.

Referring to Ferral's earlier remark that intelligence may be defined as the means of making other people, or things, do what we want Gisors counters with the suggestion that men are perhaps indifferent to the actual use of power but fascinated by the illusory possibility of doing exactly what they please. A king, he says, has the power to govern, but who wants to govern? What men want is to enforce their will—to constrain. (Government, one gathers, lies within human possibility, whereas the exercise of total constraint over another is beyond our ability.)

He continues less coherently—in short, emphatic incomplete sentences—insisting that men want most what they cannot have, to be more than men in a world of men, to escape the human condition, to be not merely powerful but omnipotent. The illness of the imagination, he goes on less vehemently and more connectedly, is the will to godhead, of which the will to power is only just an intellectual rationalization: every man dreams of being a god. A moment later he amplifies: a god can possess but cannot conquer, so that for a god the ideal would be to become a man but know at the same time that he could regain his power, whereas the dream of man is to become a god without losing his personality.

Nothing that Ferral hears helps him or us to discover exactly what Gisors takes to be the nature of the human condition, except that the will to power may be among its components. We may, if we like, conclude also that it entails enduring the limitations that keep us from becoming gods, but this is pure tautology: the trouble with being human is being human. And there are surely characters in Malraux's novel, like the pitiably humiliated Hemmelrich, who are all too human and yet not animated by the dream of becoming a god.

Is there an outside chance that Malraux may have intended Gisors's incoherence to reflect the disturbed state of the old man's mind? We have no license to assume that in other, less trying circumstances he could not have been capable of more specific, less discontinuous statement. As an ex-professor whose lectures at the University of Peking were apparently too successful for his own good, he must be up to lucid exposition. But this consideration militates against our treating him as a spokesman for Malraux.

But if he does not succeed in expounding his idea of the human condition, he has no difficulty at all in conveying how he feels about it: for him it is a source of extreme psychic discomfort. Twice his language treats it as if it were a prison or a trap, an image that has led some to see a similarity between Malraux's sensibility and that of Pascal. In his later writings Malraux would prefer to make *condition humaine* the object of verbs like "surmount" or "transcend," but, the one he puts in Gisors's mouth here is "escape."

Escape, indeed, but by what means? Gisors tells Ferral that one should intoxicate oneself—as China does with opium, Islam with hashish, and the West with sex. Even as he says this, he thinks of the ways his friends have chosen: murder, for the terrorist Tchen; love, for Kyo's wife May; inane buffoonery, for the *farfelu* Clappique. His words incite us to read Malraux's novel as if the characters were engaged, each in accordance with his own nature, in finding a way out of a cage or a snare. Doubtless such a reading can be defended as, at least, not entirely incorrect even though some of them—Katow for example—seem less visibly confined or entrapped than others.

But one hesitates. Gisors's use of "intoxicate" shows that he knows that he is prescribing mere palliatives. Narcotics, revolution, murder, clowning, and the rest only deaden the malaise of being human. One may become temporarily unconscious of the burdens and the hurts, but one does not escape them. The most we can hope to obtain from his prescription is a momentary psychic relief. We do not rise above the human condition any more than an anaesthetized patient rises above the pain of his surgery. We just become oblivious.

From the beginning of the story, when Tchen tells him about the murder, Gisors has appeared to be inordinately wise, rich in experience, and perceptive. We know him to have been modeled, in part, on two men whom Malraux respected greatly: Bernard Groethuysen, and Fernand Malraux, the writer's father. Granted; but even though one is persuaded that in other novels—in particular *L'Espoir* and *Les Noyers de l'Altenburg*—Malraux puts his own ideas in the mouths of various characters, much supports the argument that, despite Gisors's great qualities, he does not do so in this case.

In the first instance where a character in one of Malraux's novels mentions the human condition, Perken says: "Ce qui pèse sur moi, c'est ma condition d'homme." He is one of those people who take thirty years to die. From the day when he first observed the decline of his physical powers he has waited for the end. Now his wound has become virulently infected and days of bumping over a jungle track in a springless cart have exhausted his strength. No one doubts what his phrase means: he is equating "condition d'homme" with human mortality. With it the notion that Malraux was much obsessed by death and saw the bone beneath the skin entered our critical folklore.

In contrast, Gisors manages to get through the dialogue with Ferral without even a passing reference to the inevitability of death. Possibly in his sizing-up of Ferral he sees that an obsession with death is alien to the man's character. Or perhaps, in his old man's serenity, he is less than obsessed by it himself. But if he were expressing the author's own summation of the human condition, is it likely that Malraux would have neglected to have him mention it?

I find it equally hard to believe that Gisors speaks on behalf of his creator when he advocates turning to various anodynes as avenues of escape. Admittedly, gossip has long insisted that Malraux was dependent upon habit-forming drugs, but the question is less whether the rumor is founded upon fact than whether anyone as jealous of his personal privacy as Malraux was known to be would have wanted to foster such a tidbit. On the other hand, the idea could come very naturally to the mind of an inveterate opium smoker like Gisors. After all, and even though Malraux has allowed his behavior to vary from what we had been led to expect, as a self-conscious literary craftsman Malraux would have wanted to keep him in character. The words Gisors employs—"intoxicate" and "escape"—seem entirely appropriate to one who sees passivity to be a value. But who can imagine Malraux as a partisan of passivity? And who can imagine the Malraux of 1933 considering revolution to be equivalent to opium or hashish?

Certainly when Malraux returns to the subject of the human condition eighteen years later, in *Les Voix du silence,* passivity is far from his mind. The keynote is struggle; and in the eloquent eighth chapter the artist appears as the protagonist in an eternal agon, in which the antagonist is *la condition humaine* itself. With each masterwork that he achieves, the artist–creator emerges victorious. And the artist is obviously the champion and surrogate of Man. On occasion he is joined by other privileged human types. Malraux writes: "Chacun de nous éprouve que le saint, le sage, le héros sont des conquêtes sur la condition humaine."

Some suggestion of the importance Malraux attaches to the notion of struggle is conveyed by the fact that the eighth chapter of *Les Voix du silence* opens with a discussion of the nature of Greek tragedy in which he substitutes for condition humaine the old Greek personification of inevitability, the *Moira* of Homer which he calls *le destin.* I have discussed the probable reasons elsewhere at some length. Briefly, one has trouble in imagining struggling with an abstraction, whereas a personification does not present the same difficulty. Occasionally, as when Malraux says that le destin is everything that makes us conscious of our human condition, he seems to discriminate between the meanings of the terms, but more often than not he treats them as completely interchangeable. My own impression—that throughout the later writings, when he has the image of struggle in mind he is more likely to write le destin than la condition humaine can be verified—or rejected—by any reader so inclined.

Certain objections to the case I have been making here will occur to any reasonably alert reader. Garine, in *Les Conquérants,* does indeed turn to a life of revolutionary activity in order to palliate a corrosive awareness of the absurd—and who will say that an awareness of the absurd is not an aspect of man's fate? And do not the eighteen years that separate *La Condition humaine* from *Les Voix du silence* allow ample time for Malraux's disposition toward the whole question to have changed, so that he may have been presenting his own view through Gisors in 1933 and another one—different but equally his own—in 1951? Such objections have merit.

But it remains true of Garine that the analgesic fails: when illness and weakness take over, the absurd returns to haunt him, as Malraux's narrator perceives. And while the span of eighteen years is impressive, Malraux had been aware of the tragic struggle with le destin at least since the foreword of *Le Temps du mépris,* hardly a year after the publication of *La Condition humaine,* and he likewise viewed the artist as protagonist in his essay, "L'art est une conquête" which also appeared at this time (1934, in *Commune*). If he changed his mind, he did so in a remarkably short space of time.

One further consideration seems to me conclusive: Gisors's words about the human predicament simply do not sound like Malraux. Veteran readers need no reminding of the great value that Malraux always ascribed to consciousness or of his almost visceral persuasion that the more acutely conscious we are, the more intensely we are alive. One recalls how, in *La Tentation de l'Occident*—a text in which what he then calls the absurd already sounds like le destin of his later years—his young European, "A," declares that if he must live in the absurd he is determined at least to do so lucidly. And the somewhat Barrèsian exchange between Scali and Garcia in *L'Espoir:* "Dites donc, commandant, qu'est-ce qu'un homme peut faire de mieux de sa vie, pour vous?—"Transformer en conscience une expérience aussi large que possible, mon bon ami." The discussion of classical tragedy that opens the eighth chapter of *Les Voix du silence* attributes our fascination with these works to the Greeks' consciousness of our human servitude and their simultaneous ability to found our human grandeur upon it. The spectator, Malraux says, feels that the human has turned about and confronted the forces of which heretofore he has been only the plaything, and that the World of Consciousness has intruded upon "le Monde du Destin."

Even more compelling evidence of the paramount importance of consciousness for Malraux is the fact that, as the same eighth chapter builds to a climax, this quality becomes not only an intellectual value but also a pretext (in Jean Hytier's sense) for lyricism. The verbal strategies of the following paragraph are those that are called into play whenever Malraux's prose verges on the poetic. Its burden is the celebration of human consciousness itself.

Chacune des voix devient l'écho d'un pouvoir humain tantôt maintenu, tantôt obscur, et souvent disparu. En lui le désir épars

du monstre de rêves s'ordonne en images souveraines, et le cauche-
mar saturnien prend figure de rêve secourable et pacifié. Il plonge
dans le temps aussi profondément que l'homme du sang, et c'est
lui qui fait rêver à la première nuit glacée où une sorte de gorille
se sentit mystérieusement le frère du ciel étoilé. Il est l'éternelle
revanche de l'homme.

Malraux's valorization of consciousness contrasts radically with the
advice he makes Gisors give Ferral in *La Condition humaine,* to the effect
that since no man can alter his condition—and few can bear it—we do well
to turn to whatever will blunt the edge of our consciousness of it. On the
contrary, it can be surmounted as the artist-hero surmounts it in his masterpiece, while the rest of us participate in such a victory of the human.
This is the message of *Les Voix du silence.*

The message does not fully convince us, and I see what I think to be
evidence that by the time he was to write *La Métamorphose des dieux,* it did
not fully convince Malraux either. For despite the new discussion of tragedy
in *Le Surnaturel,* the vision of the artist as tragic protagonist becomes extremely faint in the last writings on art, although it does not fade out
completely. Malraux may still cherish it, but his emphasis falls elsewhere.

Other topics now exert a prior claim to his attention. Such concepts
as "englobant" and "imaginaire" (both used as nouns), which come to
figure importantly in his central argument, appear in the text at first ten-
tatively, then confidently and often. The notion of realms of being, already
useful to philosophers from Plato to Santayana, enters the discussion in
such forms as "World of Appearance," "World of Art," or "World of
Metamorphosis." Metamorphosis, on the workings of which the possibility
of an imaginary museum depends, is never long absent. And meanwhile,
le destin, although mentioned on occasion, no longer lurks, prowling and
growling, behind every chef-d'oeuvre.

Struggle of a sort, or at least confrontation, retains a paramount importance—but it is not struggle between the artist and le destin. "J'ai tenté
de rendre intelligible le monde, pour la première fois victorieux du temps,
des images que la création humaine a opposées au temps," Malraux writes
in the introduction to *Le Surnaturel.* He repeats the phrase in the special
introduction to *L'Irréel;* with slight differences in phrasing it already figures
in that of the one-volume *Métamorphose des dieux* of 1957. In all three, *le
temps* has displaced *le destin.*

To my knowledge Malraux never sat down and wrote out a list of the
components of the human condition. Since he claims that the subject of all
his books—novels, art essays, and *antimémoires*—has been nothing else, why

should he have done so? Simply by observation one concludes that in his last years the principal ones were time, history, death, and the "World of Appearance," if only because he reverts to these so often. When he writes le temps without a qualifier he means what he calls "chronological" time, measured by clock and calendar—the time of history and contingency, and of the World of Appearance. Opposed to chronological time he puts the time of the World of Art. Twice he introduces the idea that a work of art may enjoy a kind of multiple existence. A Romanesque sculpture, for example, exists in the time of the artist who created it, of the modern who views it, and in the eternity that the nature of the work posits. Art escapes the time that we do not. Otherwise the Imaginary Museum would be unimaginable.

Malraux's antihistoricism is chronic. He had written in *Les Voix du silence* that art is an *anti-destin;* now, at the end of his life, he writes that art is an *anti-histoire.* Significantly, *L'Homme précaire et la littérature* opens with his attack on the historical approach to literature practiced in the universities. And he still held *in extremis* that the most historically-minded of centuries— "the critical nineteenth"—was also the one that came nearest to accepting and being reconciled to the human condition. His tone, as he says this, is hardly one of approval.

Death, he now insists, presents two aspects: *le trépas,* which he takes in the etymological sense of "passing beyond," the event of dying; and *la mort,* apparently the opposite of being alive, thus a condition. He does not enlarge on the distinction, but one takes it that the second is the kind of death that is negated by the great work of art.

And finally, confinement to the World of Appearance would appear to mean confinement to the world of the transitory, a world ruled by chronological time.

The contexts in which some of these expressions occur in *L'Irréel* and *L'Intemporel* illumine their meaning. Here are a half-dozen from *L'Irréel:* "cette vierge devient une jeune déesse, une femme libérée da la condition humaine"; "l'art n'avait délivré de la condition humaine"; "libérer des figures mortelles de leur état de créatures"; "délivrés du monde des créatures"; "des figures créés par les vivants dans un cosmos affranchi de la création comme le héros est affranchi de la condition humaine dans le monde de l'art . . . où ils échappent ensemble à la mort"; "l'art ne transfigure pas ces personnages selon les rêves des peintres, il les délivre de la condition humaine." And in *L'Intemporel:* "Se délivrer de l'apparence"; "délivrer du temps"; "délivrance du temps"; "assemblés dans un ordre qui les émancipe du temps"; "libérer du temps."

Liberate, deliver, emancipate, *affranchir:* Malraux's vocabulary now suggests that he has come to feel the human situation as a bondage. This is not entirely new, of course. He speaks of our servitude in *Les Voix du silence,* but he does so there only briefly and in passing, whereas here he plays variations on the theme, returning to it repeatedly and insistently. Obviously this servitude differs from the hopeless penal servitude of Gisors and Pascal: the words imply the possibility of rescue. The rescuer is the artist.

But who is rescued? Not, quite plainly, the viewer of the painting or, almost as plainly, the artist; it is the virgin, the mortal figures, the figures created by living men, these personages who are transported out of the world of time and appearance—and of contingency, history and death—into the world of art. The artist must content himself with having been the instrument of the metamorphosis, the viewer with his perception that the metamorphosis has taken place. We continue to be creatures, subject to time—our acts becoming history, each of us awaiting his turn to die. Our *condition d'homme* weighs upon us as it does upon Perken. We all feel a need to escape like old Gisors. And we do not escape.

I have contended earlier that Malraux's deep addiction to figurative language marks him as something of a poet. This addiction makes him easy to misread, particularly at the times—which are anything but rare—when he seems unconcerned with whether his use of a word or phrase is figurative or literal, and even more so when, having already used a word in what one takes to be its literal sense, he uses it again in a way that makes one suspect a figurative meaning of having slipped insidiously in. Such slippages enhance the dangers of misreading because, as we all have observed, the more importance he assigns to a word or formula the less likely he is to say exactly what he means by it. Thus it is essential to recognize the metonymy here, meaning metonymy in the simple sense of the substitution of one name for another. When he writes of conquering, or surmounting, or even transcending, or being delivered from le destin or la condition humaine, he replaces a cluster of objectively verifiable facts—such as mortality, time, and history—by the malaise or psychic discomfort they cause us.

No dictionary of psychiatric terms I have been able to consult has a name for so generalized a disorder, possibly because one so widely shared cannot be considered pathological. It is easy to believe, however, that Sartre's Roquentin would see a manifestation of it in the nausea that mere living causes him. And Henri Peyre reports that in an interview Malraux laid heavy emphasis upon an *angoisse* that goes with being alive.

Now nothing can extricate us from our human condition, but we can do something to ease our chronic mental and emotional stress. For if art is an *anti-destin* or an *anti-histoire* only figuratively, it can (although Malraux does not say so) be quite literally an *anti-angoisse*.

The spectator at a Greek tragedy, Malraux has urged, did not go home from the play in a mood of dejection but in one of exaltation of the spirit. What affected him was not the bloody horror tale of the myth but the victory that the poem celebrates of the human over le destin. Similarly the virgin in the painting, according to Malraux, seems to the viewer to have put off her mortality and become a goddess; and the viewer feels that, like the spectator of the tragedy, he has witnessed the victory of art over the human condition. In more literal language than Malraux habitually uses, we may say that spectator and viewer have experienced an emotion that offsets or even overpowers their angoisse, and that allows them—in this sense—to bear their human condition.

All we learned from the Gisors-Ferral scene is that few men can stand up to their condition, that it may entail the will to constrain others, and that we should "intoxicate" ourselves. In other words, it merely adumbrates an idea that Malraux will mediate and refine during the rest of his life. That it wrote it is an important item in his intellectual biography, but I doubt that the scene adds to either our understanding or our enjoyment of the novel.

André Malraux on Revolution: Elements in *The Conquerors* and *Man's Fate*

Roger Dial

As a thinker, André Malraux has remained a very considerable enigma. It is a condition which has been cultivated by the author himself in a life that has, figuratively speaking, manufactured two biographies: one, a more or less existential search for the self in which Malraux has plundered all and any clues irrespective of isms; and the other, a life of purposeful deception—defending the self of the first biography from both the outside world and the inner truth, which Malraux came to call the "human condition." He has been or could be labeled an existentialist, a Marxist, a nihilist, an anarchist, a metaphysicist, and even a Buddhist, and not without justification in each case, for his philosophical identity has drifted subtly from one fictional ultra-ego to another over the immense chasms of ideas and epistemology resident in each of these systems of thought.

Perhaps the safe conclusion would be to label Malraux as "none of the above," and concede him to be simply "Malrauvian." But that would surely evade the most interesting aspects of his life and mind, enigmas that beg to be tackled in their makings rather than in their finished states. Equally unfruitful would be to sum him up as simply a great synthesizer. Malraux certainly did rub alien ideas together in his mind, creating co-existing theoretical contradictions. In lesser writers, such contradictions are often seen as shortcomings, but in Malraux's case they are more likely to be taken as seminal paradoxes. Thus he has given us characters as diverse as Garine and Katov, Chen and Chengtai, Gisors and Clappique; each authentic and

From *Mélanges Malraux Miscellany* 14, no. 1 (Spring 1982). © 1982 by Walter G. Langlois.

true, each a reflection to some extent of Malraux himself(s). He was all of
the isms mentioned above, and yet none of them; pieces engaged in a tolerant
eclecticism, a holistic life, but not a synthetic whole.

This leads me to Kyo, the half-breed hero of *Man's Fate,* who is, in
my judgement, so indistinctly Malrauvian because he is so distinctly synthetic, or at least the result of an attempted synthesis. In this essay I hope
that I can delineate the two sides of Kyo and the consequences of a synthesized Kyo for Malraux's pursuit of an empirically credible theory of
revolution. I will briefly speculate on Malraux's motives for attempting an
uncharacteristic synthesis; however I have no first-hand revealing insights
into his biography, and Malraux has thrown his serious biographers enough
false clues to make any proposition about his motives debatable. And finally
I will somewhat more confidently offer the judgement that the synthesis
was a failure, to some extent for the reader, the litmus of authenticity, and
surely for Malraux the seeker of a self. But first, Malraux on Revolution,
for the experiment known as Kyo is a relatively late arrival.

A PSYCHO-INDIVIDUAL THEORY OF REVOLUTION

Immersed, as we are, in an era of overlapping paradigms for life which
have in common an empirical outlook, and in which the dominant understanding of revolution is social and materialistic, it is worth reminding
ourselves that revolution can be understood in other terms as well. I have
identified Malraux's perspective as psycho-individualistic. This distinction
between the individualistic and psychological perspective, on one hand, and
the materialist and social one, on the other hand, can scarcely be more
fundamental. As correctly seen by his Marxist critics, Malraux's interpretation posits the motive force of revolution in the minds (or psychological
needs) of the individual man, attributing to human beings a power that is
free of the constraints of time or socioeconomic conditions. Nor can Malraux's conception of revolution be neatly subsumed by the historical ma-
terialists; that is, as a theory of the superstructure. For Malraux, the
revolution comes when a certain combination of individuals *needs* to be
revolutionaries. Contrary to the Marxian perspective, their alienation is as
likely to be rooted in the thesis as the antithesis side of the discernible
material contradictions of the era. If nothing else (and there is much more)
Malraux offers an explanation as to why, for the most part, the heroic
revolutionary figures of proletarianism have been decidedly bourgeois in
their personal histories.

The force underlying the psychological need of each individual has been identified by Malraux as the human condition. The concept itself is metaphysical in general, and may be informed by Buddhism in particular. There is certainly nothing material in Malraux's sense of the human condition. He writes: "The essence of man is anguish, the consciousness of his own fatality, from which all fears are born, even the fear of death (itself)" "The mind conceives man only in the eternal, and the consciousness of life can be nothing but anguish." Life, then, becomes a kind of absurd enterprize; at best an obsessed exercise in denying the undeniable fatality of existence, and more often merely suffering, amidst a "sense of exasperated impotence."

As we shall see, denying the undeniable is the only merit Malraux finds in life. "Humanity (is) a slave to absurd impulses." Behind the absurdity lay what Malraux fictioned as the "oldest Chinese legend—men are the vermin of the earth." All suffer, misery is ubiquitous and classless, we are all possessed by the idea of death and burdened by an "intense religious anxiety." Echoing not a few Conradian inventions, a Malraux character crys " 'Oh, the horror of youth!' How long before he would say 'Oh, the horror of age!' and pass on to his wretched offspring those two perfect expressions of life?" Malraux concludes that "death is no worse than life," thus offering no recommendation for either.

There is in Malraux's thinking as expressed in these two novels a distinction between life and "real life." The horror of the human condition does not necessarily move one from the former to the latter. There is no close order inspection in Malraux's novels of those who "merely live"; perhaps he couldn't quite imagine the details of such an existence. Rather, it is in the struggle of those who pursue a real life that we get a hint of the gloomy alternative. External definition of identity seems to be the common plight of those who just live. The masses are defined by their work and alienated from (real) life because of it. No less threatened is Ferral, the capitalist entrepreneur, who strives "to be distinct from his activity . . . superior to it." Or Valerie, Malraux's prototype feminist, who asserts: "It is not always easy for me to protect myself from the idea people have of me." Throughout Malraux there is an existentialist's penchant for finding real life in what one does, but an anarchist's resistance to an external-cum-social definition of that activity. The arch-Malrauvian characters of *The Conquerors* and *Man's Fate,* Garine and Chen, respectively, are consciously anti-social, precisely because the functionally integrated society is to them a cover-up of the human condition, a collective life within fatality, not a real life resisting it. Only when engaged in revolution—that is, the dismantlement of society—are men *collectively* capable of sensing real life. It is worth noting that this idea will be contradicted briefly by Malraux through the character May at the end of *Man's Fate* as he laboriously argues for the Stalinist prescription that socialist labor is part of, not the end of, the revolution. Intellectually, Malraux may have escaped this for a time, but intuitively Chen, as Garine before him, denies it; *class* consciousness outside the maelstrom of revolution is no consciousness at all.

Before pursuing real life, however, man must somehow come to know of the human condition. Society, the guardian of the lie, may itself over-direct the imitation drama, rendering in the individual an irritation with "supernumerary parts . . . giving one a sense of being a walkon thrust on stage by some obscure motivation in a play of unusually spurious psychology performed for a stupid audience." Alternatively, society is less the enemy than the enemy's stand-in. At first "you think it's something to fight off, something outside you (but) the disease is your*self*" (emphasis Malraux's). The sickness metaphor appears throughout these novels, signalling the existential crises that must be endured and re-endured as one strives to make a real life.

Society is less likely to catalyse an existential crisis than is its opposite, solitude. In solitude there is the unwanted prospect of contemplation. Old Gisors, from *Man's Fate,* speaks for (and of) many Malrauvian characters: "All suffer, and each one suffers because he thinks." And, of course, the horrific thought that is likely to fill the vacuum of solitariness is the idea of death. Malrauvians are "overwhelmed by the discovery of death," they are "alone with death," they "feel death," "the idea of death puts things into perspective" for them. With this, the existential crisis bottoms out, and the tide may be turned psychologically. "One can communicate even with death . . . it's most difficult, but perhaps it's the meaning of life." Malrauvians all learn that "they only have one life to live"; out of context, a rather sanguine cliché, but in the overall Malrauvian vision, a bitter fortune, an offer one dare not refuse.

Finally, the existential crisis can be purposefully induced; it can be an object of revolutionary pedagogy. Malraux likens the process to fatherhood. Rebecci created Hong, Gisors spiritually fathered Chen, and Garine—the master propagandist—spawned a whole generation of coolies, revealing to them "that they exist, just that they exist." The father figures, of course, were in each case commiting their scion to certain misery, to a state of deep psychological suffering. But one way or the other, at some point most people are felled by the existential crisis. The metaphor favored by Malraux is illness: "sick people are nothing unusual." As a writer he catalogues a multitude of prescriptions and tonics, often using existential phraseology:

"What is hardest is to know what you want." A real life of one sort or another is the only tonic for the human condition, and as we shall see some of these tonics are by purpose or consequence revolutionary. For want of a better word we shall refer to these tonics as existential resurrections, and deal with the epistemological snags in the concept as we proceed. For one who comes to know the human condition, some form of existential resurrection is "necessary," instinctively as necessary as gasping is to a drowning man. Knowledge of the human condition foretells a struggle: epic in its proportions relative to simply living, generally tragic in its outcome, and always heroic in the performance.

"The only way to fight back is to create something." The something which Malraux has in mind is, in fact, no "thing" at all, but a "self." "At the centre of all misery there's often a man. You have to hang on to that man after the misery's licked. That is not easy." In the existentialist mode Malraux assures us that finding and hanging on to that man is a matter of individual choice. Malrauvian heroes "serve the gods of their choice," and the most fulfilled heroes serve themselves as godheads. Symbolically, the resurrection of the self happens by degrees, often spurred on by recurring crisis encounters with the human condition, and aided by searching stares into mirrors (Garine) and a growing consciousness of the other unrecognizable voice in the throat (Kyo and Gisors). Altogether, the struggle takes a lifetime to complete—no less, no more—and optimally Malraux sees such a life as the "noble figure of a victim (of the human condition) supervising his own biography."

Within that illusive self, men find ideas and a will to action. Malraux's heroes flee from the human condition into a life of action rationalized by some great—though not necessarily noble—idea. The object is to "bind yourself to any great line of action and not back off." The substance of action is, of course, irrelevant to Malraux's psychological thesis, though acts of obedience, murder, and conquest are particularly salient to occurrence of revolution. Nor is Malraux wont to judge the ideas men choose to follow from any standard save their utility in the essential struggle of all life: that against mortality. From the revolutionary perspective, however, some are more salient than others, and the contest between ideas generally becomes one of the more interesting planes of revolution, even for Malraux. In the discussion of characters below we will look at the impact of several riveting ideas dredged from the selfhoods of Malrauvian heroes. Ideas such as equality, selflessness, justice, dignity, fraternity, nation, class, power, et cetera. What is crucial is not the content, but the obsessive hold of the idea. It must become a virtual fetish in one's existence; one must live within its intensity and "carry it to the extreme" at the level of action. Malraux likens the power of an idea to a religious life of daily conversion. To be psychologically effective there can be little room for subtlety: "stubborn drive" is what is essential. "If you live this real life to fight that (pause) other life, you can't do it full of private yearnings." Malrauvian heroes are sure of *something*, it doesn't matter what. Nor does it matter if they are right. Katov, in *Man's Fate*, for example, prefaces every statement with the confident adjective "absolutely."

What, then, does Malraux conceive to be the culmination of this life against death struggle? Is denying the undeniable merely an exercise in self-deception—mere illusion to get the individual through the pain of existence? And if this is so, how can he call this illusion real life? I think it is safe to say that the final bead in Malraux's conceptual rosary is not so much a shade of nihilist black as a hue of eastern saffron. To be sure, he persists in doubting the reality of anything except death; nor does his view contain the promise of transcendent resurrection, save that occasionally contained in the memory of martyrdom. But if not ultimately resurrected, his heroes—or at least the "winners" among them—do transcend the human condition in a metaphysically real sort of way. Originally fleeing from death, Malraux's heroes long for sleep, for "universal serenity," to relax, or to be lost in a "halo of indifference." Longing is actualized at first in a momentary illusion of being free, a sense of "that indescribable wholeness that lets us feel our lives as good for something." We are perhaps still in the realm of self-deception, as Chen, of *Man's Fate*, was when he felt himself drifting "nearer the sky" or when "it seemed to Gisors that the wind was passing through him like a river, like Time itself, and for the first time the idea that Time, which was bringing him closer to death, was flowing through him (and) did not isolate him from the world, but joined him to it in a serene accord." But in a qualitative sense we leave the realm of self-deception and enter a kind of amorphous reality of metaphysical truth as Gisors probes the depths of his self and of his essential anxiety: "Just as Kyo had not recognized his own voice because he had heard it with his throat, so he—Gisors—probably could not reduce his consciousness of himself to that which he could have of another person, because it was not acquired by the same means. It owed nothing to the senses. (Yet) he felt himself penetrating into a domain which belonged to him more than any other. With his intruding consciousness he was anxiously treading a forbidden solitude where no one would ever join him. For a second he had the sensation that it was THAT which must escape death."

Through Gisors, however, we do not quite make it to Malraux's promised land; the old man is tragically tied to life by parenthood and must find his (incomplete) relief in opium. Gisors is a loser, and it is to the winners that we must look to grasp the fragile promise of transcending the human condition offered by Malraux. He has told us that the only way to fight back is to create something, and that the "something" is the self, actualized through a real life. But a real life is incomplete without a meaningful death—"to die on the highest possible plane." Again there is no content to the prescription: the self, not Malraux the author or the witnesses of a life, determines what the highest plane must be. Ideally, a "death must resemble life"; there must be a continuity of meaning, and it is this continuity that preserves the self, not only against the fear of mortality but against mortality itself. Gisors, ever the seer, never the achiever, philosophizes: "Every man is a madman . . . but what is human destiny if not a life of effort to unite this madman and the universe . . . every man dreams of being god." Malraux has given us a few who succeed, not by clinging to illusions, but by probing deeper and discovering the kernel of self that unifies life and death, and by this enactment of godhead he nullifies the human condition—denies fate.

It is within these ubiquitous and timeless dynamics of existential crisis and resurrection that Malraux fashions a political theory of revolution in general, and a political analysis of the Chinese revolution in particular. Revolutions occur, and succeed or fail, when men respond to the human condition, and respond in particular ways. The individual and the psychological are the analytic starting points to his understanding of the minutest levels of behavioural action and the macro sweeps of history. His theory of revolution moves from the "Individual Parts" to the "Conqueror's Framework."

THE INDIVIDUAL PARTS

The revolutionary landscape of these two novels is seeded with many exquisite individual characters. Though the novel form necessitates that some play larger roles than others, one easily senses that for Malraux they are of equal interest (indeed, virtue), for it is not the variety of what they do that interests the author nearly so much as the commonality of why they act at all. It is through that universal plight that Malraux communes so personally with characters who are otherwise as diverse as the terrorist Hong and Chengtai the pacifist whom he needs to murder.

Few characters could be more quintessentially Malrauvian than Hong in *The Conquerors*. His existential crisis is explicit: "Bound to the present by his overwhelming discovery of death," his existential resurrection is characterized by a prolonged process of self-discovery. "For some time now an unusual personality has been working to Hong's surface . . . a new personality . . . wholly ruled by the violence of his nature and of youth, and by the only way of life he truly knows—poverty." Malraux's interest in "poverty" in this context is not a matter of economic systems or material concerns. It is the psychological humiliation that poverty makes probable which is salient, because "deep humiliation calls for violent negation of the world . . . and only blood insistently shed can feed such solitudes." In fact Hong denies having any interests: "he accepts nothing, seeks nothing, discusses nothing: he hates." It is this hate alone that makes Hong part of the revolution; he wants no role in the outcome or the planning of an outcome. "All social order is a lot of shit. A man's one life. Not to throw it away. That's all." "Every murder boosts his self-confidence and he's learning what he really is, deep down: an anarchist." And in the almost perfect Malrauvian conclusion to an individual life, Hong leads a life that resembles death; merging the two, he swears to die for the idea that has been his life, and thereby escape the human condition. Like Sartre's Hugo in *Dirty Hands,* Hong needs only to die in the exercise of his hate. Executed by the Revolutionary organization, Hong is tragically deprived of his culminating deserts.

The seasoned revolutionary soldier of the International, Katov is the antithesis of Hong; his part in the revolution is not hate, but fraternal life. Yet the psychological route he has travelled to discover this essence of his selfhood is very similar to that travelled by Hong. Exiled to the Siberian labor camps, he came face to face with his mortality. "He knew from experience that the worst suffering is in solitude." "The main thing is not to be alone," he consoles Himmelrich. Nursed out of his hopeless state by a simple peasant wife, Katov identifies the idea—love—around which he could construct his defense against the human condition. Katov becomes a "believer in the virtues of the heart"; his life becomes an expression of "limitless tenderness" and "manly affection," and throughout the novel he "joins himself in absolute friendship" with one crisis-ridden comrade after another. In prerevolutionary times he had longed to be a doctor. Though late in discovering himself, there is no doubt that Katov has been delivered to his own essence. Katov's temporary diversions into brutality and organizational discipline find their way into his exterior appearance, but the inner man, Malraux assures us, was always something softer: "the expression of ironic ingeniousness which the small eyes and especially the upturned nose gave to Katov's face, was all the more pronounced as it jarred with his essential character." It is this most inner aspect that is Katov's gift to the revolution: "fraternity, without a face, almost without a real voice." "Through words he could do almost nothing, but beyond words there were the things which gestures, looks, mere presence were capable of expressing." Malraux's penchant for the tragic twice deprives Katov of the continuity of a fraternal life unto death: early in the novel he alone survives a firing squad, and later in the horrific scene of men being cast into the bowels of a steam engine "Katov felt himself deserted. He turned over on his belly and waited. The trembling of his shoulders did not cease."

Just as hate and love are component parts of the revolutionary situation, so are blind discipline and organizational loyalty. These too derive from the need to excape the human condition into something that is sure. For Nikolaieff, the Chekist turned Bolshevik, it is organization, per se, that does the trick. His mortality is neutralized by its immortality, as with the career soldier in many an army. Similarly, Vologin in *Man's Fate* escapes into the crudest determinism of Marxist dialectics (as interpreted by the Party). Merging himself into that fatality, he is able to proceed with life— and revolutionary action—with assurity. "Obedience to the Party is the only logical attitude," he recites. In the works of so many otherwise fine novelists, characters such as Nikolaieff and Vologin could be nothing more than reprehensible stereotypes, cardboard martinets. But Malraux has informed these characters with a psychological thesis that makes their lives a meaningful answer (no better, no worse) to a universal dilemma. Their effect on the revolution is still up for judgement; but since they have motivation, their lives have a third dimension, and they possess a reality which can not be dismissed without a certain amount of empathy. Malraux would say that they have chosen the right vice, the vice that is appropriate to their psychological needs and is consistent with their essential selves.

It is important to Malraux that men choose the right vice, that they choose an obsession that releases them from the suffering of the human condition in a sustained fashion. Not everyone does, of course. Perhaps few do. And thus there is no guarantee that life, even in the crucible of revolution, will move to selfhood and salvation. Still, these tragic existences play parts in the revolutionary situation and beg consideration.

Clappique, the mythomanic "Punchinello" or "Fantômas" of *Man's Fate* is one such tragic character. His double-meaning motto: "Baron de Clappique does not exist" (is he a baron?) signals a great sensitivity to the human condition. Amazed, he asks why everybody isn't a mythomaniac; how anyone can survive without a "plastic point of view." Clappique lives by denying life and "lives inadequately by it" because the fantastic forms he assumes with the aid of alcohol cannot be sustained for long. But in the interim he is capable of becoming "drunk with his lie, with the fictive world he creates . . . a world where truth no longer exists." In his fantasies Clappique is able to pretend that he does not exist (contrast to Gisors, who in the Buddhist sense really believes that there is no existence except suffering), and when awakened from these flights he is moved to find another surrogate reality, where the human condition can be touched, without allowing it to touch back with all of its force. In the gambling house Clappique has "the feeling of seizing life." Here is "the only means he had found of possessing himself." Of course, it is neither life nor himself that he discovers in Gambling, but rather the "frenzy of losing," an imitation encounter with death. Unfortunately for him, Clappique is too intelligent not to recognize the real motivation in gambling: "It is r-remarkable how people can say that the player's sensation is caused by his hope of winning! It's as if they said that men fight duels to become fencing champions." Thus Clappique lives out his life perpetually at the edge of existential crisis, unable to find in himself the makings of salvation. Malraux suggests that Clappique may be a rare creature wherein resides no essence, no self, the object of a preordained damnation. None the less, Clappique's efforts at fending off the human condition have consequences for the revolution. The fantasizing of adventure contributes daring to the cause; the pathos of gambling results in betrayal of the cause.

Gisors, the old philosopher, is another Malrauvian whose life is a pursuit of the wrong vices. By profession and nature he is a solitary and contemplative man, and because of this he has come to know "the anguish and obsession of death." His pursuit of a selfhood is complicated by many false clues; he sees elements of his own personality in everybody he knows and ponders the possibility of having several selves. Malraux uses some familiar symbolic devices to capture Gisors's pursuit of the illusive inner being: "I have had the experience of finding myself unexpectedly before a mirror and not recognizing myself." He is "unable to recognize his own voice." If Gisors has an essence, it is love of son (Kyo), not in the selfish dynastic sense (he knows that "he could not escape from himself into another being"), but in a singularly altruistic sense. This is Gisors's essence and his tragedy, for—as the Greeks knew—the reciprocal love between men— fraternity—does not necessarily apply to the son-father relationship. Thus Gisors is bound to life, not freed from it, by his essence. For a time he attempts to relieve the anguish of his special entrapment in the human condition through the idea of Marxism; in his view, as he says, Marxism was "a fatality, and I found myself in harmony with it because my fear of death was in harmony with fatality." It is an inadequate belief, an intensity that is somehow false and unsure. In the presence of his son, Gisors is always reminded that he is "interested in individuals instead of forces." The death of his son provides Gisors with the first real opportunity he has had to operationalize the essential truth which opium has allowed him to flirt with, without entirely embracing. "Marxism has ceased to live in me . . . there is hardly any fear left in me. Since Kyo died I am indifferent to death. I am freed from both life and death. . . . One can fool life for a long time, but in the end it always makes us what we were intended to be. Every old man is a confession, believe me, and if old age is usually so empty it is because the men themselves were empty and managed to conceal it . . . men should be able to learn that there is no reality." Gisors has learned his essence is that of a bodhi-sattva. "His eyes shut, carried by great motionless wings (he) contemplates his solitude: a desolation that joined the divine, while, at the same time, the wave of serenity that gently covered the depths of death widened into infinity."

Men such as Gisors, Hong, Clappique and Vologin, then, are the lowest common denominators of the revolutionary situation. They are alienated from life by a sense of the human condition and energized into particular forms of mind and action by the essence of their deepest selfhood. Acting alone, however, they do not give direction to revolution. Typically, revolutions have frameworks: purpose or organization (though not necessarily both). As we shall see through the character Chen, Malraux may have come to doubt even this. But before his mind carried him to the ambiguities of Chen, Malraux was convinced that central to all revolutions there was a "tough minded minority" whose role was to give direction to revolution. As one such individual—Garine—said: "We are the framework."

THE CONQUEROR'S FRAMEWORK

The phenomena of political leadership, in revolutions or otherwise, are ubiquitous enough that no political theory is complete without some accounting for them. Marxism, of course, has its notion of the vanguard, in the Marxist era a Party-based elite that emerges from (or at least represents) the most conscious social elements of the antithesis classes. Malraux's elites, on the other hand, materialize out of no such social or historical schema. They are, like all Malrauvians, individuals in flight from the human condition. What makes them different from the majority is that their essential character requires that their existential resurrection become a conquest of others. Having power is their personal antidote to the mortality crises they face. But power does not exist in a vacuum, free for the wanting or needing. Power has to be taken from others or built out of chaos. Garine assures us: "Anarchy, old buddy, is when government (a matrix of power) is weak, not when there is no government at all. In the first place, there is always government; when things go badly, there is more than one, that's all." These elites are "the Conquerors." By seizing power they alter social and political systems—they are, then, revolutionaries. In order to achieve or secure power they must impose themselves on others, the disparate individualistic parts discussed above. The exact form of conquest, of course, varies with the essential selves of the conquerors. But the object of conquest is the same: "an urge to compel. To be more than a man, in a world of men. To escape man's fate . . . Not powerful, all-powerful. The visionary disease, of which the will to power is only the intellectual justification, is the will to god-head: every man dreams of being god."

Malraux began his explorations of the Conqueror-type with the character of Pierre Garine. Garine's awareness of the human condition was catalysed by his entrapment in a courtroom farce, which—it is generally believed—represents Malraux's rationalization of his own trial experience in colonial Indochina. The experience leaves in Garine "a sense of exasperated impotence, scorn and disgust as in the face of a fanatical mob, as in all large-scale manifestations of human absurdity." The "confused hopes of his adolescence," that there is goodness or ultimate purpose to be found in mankind, faded into a realization that "all life was useless, that humanity was a slave to absurd impulses." Garine can no longer love mankind, and thus he commits himself to separating himself from it in a special way: "You can live by accepting the absurd, you can't live in the absurd." This commitment is fueled by a "deep down, stubborn, persistent craving for power." His life becomes a test of the horrific hypothesis: "There is only one 'right' that isn't a joke: the most efficient use of force." "Finally he came to see the exercise of power as a sort of relief, a deliverance." "Running things. Making decisions. Controlling men. That's where life is." "Life is action . . . indifference to everything that isn't action, including the results of action." Malraux develops the character of Garine as a man struggling against disease, finding in the domination instincts of self an apparent panacea to the human condition. Garine brags of his recovery: "I have become strong putting total absence of scruples at the service of something other than my own interest." But power, ultimately, is no cure at all; "private fears" return, "the absurd reasserts its rights," and Garine teeters repeatedly at the edge of breakdown.

Garine's existential resurrection is tragically built on at least one fallacy.

Power does not free the individual; conquest is a form of service. His very substantial gift to the revolution—a belief only in energy and his capacity to organize emotions into social force—facilitates the construction of a new order in which his part can only be that of a servant. "I've always hated to 'serve'. And who's served more than I have here, or better? For years—years!—I've wanted power, and I can't even wrap my own life in it." Even at the brink of personal defeat, Garine clings desperately to his hypothesis of life: "There is still one thing that matters in life: not to be defeated." But Garine is not blind, his tragedy is probably self-conscious: "He doesn't believe in what he is saying and he's trying hard, with every raw nerve, to persuade himself. Does he know he's doomed? Is he only afraid he's doomed? Or doesn't he know anything for sure?" Thus, the other flaw in Garine's resurrection may well be his nihilism itself. We will be able to see where Malraux stands on this better in the context of Kyo.

There are other conquerors, with different frameworks to impose on society, to be found in these novels. There is Borodin, with "the vivid memory of his own adolescence—a young Jew . . . with contempt all around him." Borodin has made his commitment to "grapple with reality," to deny the human condition by reducing existence to empirical assurity. He becomes a "technician" armed with "scientific socialism," a navigator who certainly knows his ship, and thinks he knows "true north." Malraux doubts the latter, and he redeems Borodin (doubtlessly against the real character's will) for the tragic: like "Garine, the deep thinkers have been predicting his future . . . Borodin will end up the same . . . individual conscience is the real disease of leadership."

There is Chengtai, who—haunted by solitude in life and in death—commits himself to the idea of justice constructed out of nonviolence. Malraux, of course, doesn't find this idea any more plausible than Borodin's scientific socialism: "His whole life is a moral protest, and his hope of victory through justice is the most powerful outward manifestation of the ubiquitous, deep and irremediable *frailty* of his race." But from the perspective of revolution the "frailty" in his form of resurrection doesn't matter; what matters is that "like every man who sways great masses, this polite little man of polite little gestures is obsessed—obsessed by Justice. He feels that imposing Justice is his private mission; he perceives Justice vaguely as a creation of his own mind." Chengtai needs to be the "caretaker of the revolution"; it is a form of conquest in life that he manages to merge into a meaningful death as a martyr. That the force of his martyrdom comes to be used in another framework is of importance to the course of the revolution, but of no significance to Chengtai, who is one of the few personal winners. While Malraux was self-confident enough to impose (predict) his tragic metaphysical sense on Borodin, he timidly avoided anything but a political judgement of Gandhi.

These, then, are the conquerors of The Conquerors. They are the keepers of the idea of revolution, either as a set of ends or as a process. Though the origins of their action lay in the same psychological realm as everyman, their pursuit of power acts as a counter-force to the divergencies of individual flights from the human condition. Their need is to choreograph a multitude of individual flights into a social dance called "revolution." Their need for power imposes a kind of "intelligence" on the anarchy of atomized freedom searching in mankind. The bottom line of Malraux's understanding of revolution is as simple as the component parts of his thesis are complex: as the conquerors go, so goes the revolution.

THE TROTSKY CRITIQUE

Trotsky's two critical reviews of The Conquerors are, in the largest sense, irrelevant and unjustified—except at the level of revolutionary polemics. Predictably he made no attempt to understand Malraux's thesis in its own terms, and he measured the book against a yardstick (Marxism) which had nothing to do with its construction beyond casual ornamentation. The polemical exchange and the subsequent personal meeting would be nothing more than interesting historical footnotes, were it not for their apparent effect on Malraux's second analysis of the Chinese revolution.

Trotsky's critique was well-honed, intelligent within its paradigm, and predictable. To summarize, the great revolutionist found the young writer wanting on three scores. First, Malraux's revolution is all "sixes and sevens," unpredictable. This, argues Trotsky, is because the young author rejects empirical method for that of the sorcerers. "Only the study of the anatomy of society and its physiology permits one to react to the course of events by basing oneself upon scientific foresight and not upon a dilettante's conjectures." Secondly, following from the above, Malraux failed to understand the material "base" of revolution. His revolutionary hero, "the functionary adventurer, raises himself above all the classes of the Chinese nation. He considers himself predestined to dominate, to give orders, to command, independently of the internal relationships of forces in China." Malraux's understanding of revolution, thus, lacked what Trotsky called "social vigor." And finally, "the book is lacking in a congenital affinity between the writer, despite all he knows, understands and can do, and his heroine, the revolution." Trotsky recommends a corrective—"a good inoculation of Marxism would have preserved the author." Trotsky reverses himself in the last line of the final exchange: "In my (first) article I expressed the idea that an inoculation of Marxism would do Garine (Malraux) good. I don't think so anymore."

One cannot think of too many cases in which an author answers such critics by carrying their advice, positively, into a subsequent work. It would be beyond my competence to develop a biographically specific, causal argument here. Suffice it to say that it seems evident that Trotsky's voice had an authority and poignancy which spoke directly to a weakness of epistemological confidence in Malraux. *Man's Fate* is indelibly an attempt to reflect elements of Trotsky's materialism and empiricism, if not ultimately his viewpoint. Through the characters Kyo, Suan, and Pei Malraux revises his framework of understanding in a way that he might reasonably have expected would satisfy his Marxist critics. He may also have learned something about himself along the way. Through Gisors, Malraux accepts Trotsky's final damnation in good humor, while defending revolution outside the Marxist paradigm—his revolution!—through the character Chen.

THE REVISIONISM OF MAN'S FATE

Kyo, like all Malrauvian heroes, flees the human condition by searching deeply for the essence of his selfhood. In the early stages of his existential resurrection he comes to the "conviction that ideas were not to be thought, but lived. Kyo had chosen action." The central idea of that action was "dignity" and Kyo becomes obsessed with the delivery of dignity to all "his people." Like Garine, Kyo sets out to give meaning to his life by conquering. What is more, Kyo realizes (and achieves) the ultimate psychological feat: he neutralizes death, by making it an extension of life. "Kyo had seen much death, and helped by his Japanese education, he had always thought that it is fine to die by one's own hand, a death that resembles one's life . . . To die is passivity, but to kill oneself is action." In the final act of his life, Kyo is able to actualize this understanding: "Dying could be an exalted act, the supreme expression of a life which this death so much resembles . . . he crushed the poison between his teeth as he would have given a command." Kyo is a man in charge of his biography to the end.

Though Kyo moves dutifully through Malraux's psychological hoops, he is anything but a typical Malrauvian. His life is an expression of hope, not tragedy; his conquest, far from being illusory, is real (or potentially real). For these revisions Malraux had to reach beyond his own thesis—one might well say beyond himself. Kyo is a mixed blood, and Malraux would have us take him to be the synthesized Marxian-Malrauvian. Indeed, it is this melding of the two sides of Kyo that amounts to the discovery of his most inner self. Malraux captures the marriage of parts: "the oscillations of the (swinging) lamp became shorter and shorter: Kyo's two faces reappeared by turns, less and less different from each other." Kyo is not only an individual resisting the human condition; he becomes in Malraux's revisionist text a representative of a class of resisters: "He belonged with (the downtrodden); they had the same enemies. . . . Kyo had not tried to win them; he had sought and found his own kind." The duality is carried through to his demise: "He was dying among those with whom he would have wanted to live; he was dying because he had given meaning to his life . . . death saturated with brotherly quavering." Kyo is the *self* of the body revolution in life and in death.

It can be argued that Kyo's origins are to be found in the hole Malraux left in Garine's (Malraux's?) epistemology, a hole Trotsky catalysed Malraux to fill: "There is no power, not even any "real life", without a conviction of the world's futility—an obsession with it . . . the whole meaning of his (Garine's) life is tied to that belief . . . he draws great strength from his deep feeling that human existence is absurd. (But) *if the world isn't absurd,* then he's frittered away his life in vain gestures—not in a fundamental, exalting vanity but in the vanity of despair." As Garine neared his end, Malraux again conceded that his rejection of reality as "senseless" may have been wrong, that Garine (Malraux?) doesn't know anything for sure. Garine's life was thus a gamble, maybe even a calculated nihilist guess. Because of this epistemological void Garine is obliged to proclaim himself "asocial as I'm an atheist and in the same way. None of that would matter a damn if I were an academic, but I know I'll have to spend my life on the fringes of *some* social order, and that I'll never be able to accept it without renouncing all that I truly am."

Kyo, no less a conqueror than Garine, differs however in that he knows the world isn't absurd. He draws this knowledge from observation and from a deep intuition that he is part of a real force, a force which has both history and presence. Taking his lead directly from Trotsky, Malraux quells any suspicion that this real force might be illusionary—that is, mere doctrine. "Marxism is not a doctrine, it is a 'will'. For the proletariat and those who belong with them (Kyo), it is the will to know themselves, to feel themselves as proletarians, and to conquer as such; you must be Marxist not in order to be right, but in order to conquer without betraying yourselves." Here then is the synthesis, the simultaneous individual and collective unification of the human condition.

Trotsky also took Malraux to task for not observing the obvious fact that the Chinese proletarian, as a class alone, was far from sufficiently developed to lead the struggle against the bourgeois and imperialist domination of China. Malraux promptly assumes the objective stance of a socialist realist and gives us Suan, the ideal proletarian, and Pei, the ideal nationalist. Neither character has individual depth; they are categories out of another paradigm, where individuality could be construed to be "capricious," if not deviationist.

Up to this point it would be difficult to say that Malraux's attempt at synthesis was not a success. The tooling of Kyo was skillfully done, a minor masterpiece of logical alchemy. True, Malraux was obliged to sacrifice his (bourgeois-defeatist?) penchant for tragedy in the construction of Kyo, but he managed to give Kyo a death which was meaningful in both the Marxian paradigm and in the Malrauvian framework.

But there is something curious about the conclusion of *Man's Fate*: it does not end with Kyo, but with Gisors defining and defending his path outside the historical space of Kyo and his Marxist brethren. It is Gisors, speaking the wisdom of the East, not dialectical materialism: "The consciousness of life can be nothing but anguish . . . How many sufferings scattered about in this light would disappear, if thought were to disappear." What is more, while Kyo is generally regarded as the hero of *Man's Fate,* he shares the spotlight almost equally with Chen. Chen is, in fact, a political counterpoint to Kyo's collective side: "let each one assume a responsibility and appoint himself the judge of an oppressor's life. Give an immediate meaning to the individual without hope and multiply the attempts, not by an organization, but by an idea—revive the martyrs." The distance between this viewpoint and Marxism is later recited by Pei: "The murder of the dictator is the duty of the individual towards himself (but) must be separate from political action, which is determined by collective forces."

In the final analysis, Malraux wrote himself full circle in *Man's Fate*. He made space for materialism, empiricism, and historicism in his mind. It is even possible that he wanted this epistemology, with all its assurity, to become his vehicle out of the human condition. He demonstrated effectively that he could handle it intellectually, even aesthetically. But, to put it in Malrauvian terms, Marxism just wasn't him, and Malraux would have to work on his doubts and supervise his biography for another forty-three years after the appearance of *Man's Fate*.

Chronology

1901   Georges-André Malraux is born in Paris, November 3. His parents, Fernand Malraux and Berthe Lamy are separated in 1905. His maternal grandmother and aunt raise André in Bondy, a small suburb of Paris.

1909   Malraux's grandfather dies at Dunkirk.

1914–18   Malraux's father is conscripted.

1919   Malraux attends lectures at the Musée Guimet and the Ecole du Louvre. He is employed by the bookseller-publisher René-Louis Doyon. Begins study of Sanskrit. Meets François Mauriac.

1920   Malraux's first article, "Des origines de la poesie cubiste," is published in *La Connaissance,* a review edited by Doyon. Articles on Lautréamont and André Salmon are also published in the review *Action.* Becomes the artistic director of the publisher Simon Kra; publishes works by Remy de Gourmont, Max Jacob, Ensor, Derain, Léger, and Baudelaire.

1921   Malraux begins his friendship with Kahnweiler, who publishes his *Lunes en papier,* a surrealist work illustrated by Léger, in a limited edition of 100 copies. Other articles by Malraux are published in journals. He travels to Italy. On October 21, he marries Clara Goldschmidt.

1922   Begins acquaintance with Picasso. Articles on Gide and Jacob are published in *Action.* First article appears in *Nouvelle Revue Française (NRF),* on *L'Abbaye de Typhaines* by Gobineau.

1923   Travels to Indochina with Clara and Louis Chevasson. After visiting the Cambodian temple of Banteai-Srey, from which they remove statues and bas-reliefs, the group is accused of theft and arrested in Pnom-Penh.

1924   Trial in Pnom-Penh. Doyon, contacted by Clara, begins an appeal for Malraux's release in *L'Eclair*. Twenty-three celebrated authors sign a similar appeal, including Mauriac, Gide, and Breton. Malraux is reprieved and returns to France, where he publishes "Ecrit pour une idole à trompe" in *Accords*.

1925   Returns to Indochina and organizes the "Young Annam" movement with Nguyen Pho. Also launches, with Paul Monin, the newspaper he entitles *L'Indochine*, whose publication will cease in August due to printers' refusals to print it. In November, the paper reappears as *L'Indochine enchaînée*.

1926   In Paris Malraux directs *A la sphère*, which publishes works by Samain, Morand, Giraudoux, Gide, and Mauriac. *La Tentation de l'Occident* is published by Grasset in August.

1927   *Commerce* publishes "Le Voyage aux Iles Fortunées." The *Review 600* publishes "Ecrit pour un ours en peluche." His essay "D'une jeunesse européenne" is published in *Ecrits*.

1928   *Les Conquérants* and *Royaume farfelu* are published by Grasset and Gallimard respectively. Visits Persia. Becomes member of the Comité de Lecture as well as artistic director at Gallimard until the Spanish Civil War.

1930   Publication of *La Voie royale*. Malraux travels to Afghanistan, India, Japan, and the United States.

1931   Debate between Trotsky and Malraux at *NRF* about *Les Conquérants*. Travels to China, writes a preface to Charles Clement's *Mediterranée*.

1932   Exhibition of Gothic-Buddhist art at *NRF*. Malraux writes preface to D. H. Lawrence's *Lady Chatterley's Lover*. Meets Heidegger.

1933   Writes preface to Faulkner's *Sanctuary*. Publishes *La Condition humaine* which is a great success, and wins the Prix Goncourt in December. Daughter Florence is born.

1934   Flies over the Desert of Dhana with Edouard Corniglion-Molinier, searching for the "Kingdom of the Queen of Sheba." This adventure is described in *L'Intransigeant*. Meets with Trotsky in March. Becomes president of the World Committee for the Liberation of Dimitrov and Thaemann. Travels to Berlin with Gide to present a letter to Goebbels. Member of the Presidium of the International League against Antisemitism. President of the World Committee against War and Fascism. In August he addresses the first Congress of Soviet Writers in Moscow. Meets Meyerhof and Eisenstein (whose plans to make a film of *La Condition humaine* are halted by Stalin). Meets Gorky and Pasternak. Meets T. E. Lawrence.

1935   *Le Temps du mépris.*

1936   Speech in June at the International Congress of Writers for the Defense of Culture in London. Travels to Spain at the start of the Spanish Civil War and heads an international air squadron, fighting with the Republicans. Flies on sixty-five air missions and is twice wounded.

1937   *L'Espoir.* Travels to the United States and Canada to raise money for the Spanish Republican cause. Meets Hemingway, Einstein, and Robert Oppenheimer. Camus adapts *Le Temps du mépris* for the Théâtre du Travail in Algiers.

1938   Makes film of *L'Espoir (Sierra de Teruel)* in Barcelona, music by Darius Milhaud. "La Psychologie des Renaissances" and "De la Représentation en Occident et en Extrême-Occident" are published in *Verve.*

1939   Gallimard publishes "Etude sur Laclos." Film is finished in April and shown privately in July.

1940   Captured in Sens with his tank unit. Five months later he escapes to the free zone.

1943   *Les Noyers de l'Altenburg* published in Switzerland.

1944   Active as a Resistance leader, using the name Colonel Berger (after the hero in *Les Noyers de l'Altenburg*). Taken prisoner in Toulouse, later freed by the French. Josete Clotis, with whom Malraux had two sons, is killed in an accident. Half-brother Claude, also a member of the Resistance, is executed. Malraux is involved in the liberation of the Vosges and Alsace, especially Strasbourg.

1945   Death of another half-brother, Roland, also a member of the Resistance. Malraux becomes Minister of Information for the first De Gaulle government.

1947–50   Malraux is director of propaganda for the R.P.F. (Rassemblement de peuple francais), the Gaullist party. He publishes essays on art, *La Psychologie de l'art.* Marries Madeleine Malraux, widow of his half-brother Roland.

1951   *Les Voix du silence.*

1952–54	*Le Musée imaginaire de la sculpture mondiale* published in three volumes.
1957	*La Metamorphose des dieux,* volume 1.
1958	Malraux is Minister of Information in the second De Gaulle government.
1959–69	Malraux is Minister of Cultural Affairs.
1961	An automobile accident kills both of Malraux's sons, Pierre-Gauthier and Vincent.
1962–63	Malraux travels to the United States twice. He is a guest of the Kennedys at the White House.
1965	Malraux suffers acute depression. Travels to China and other Asian countries. Resumes writing.
1966	Reunion with poet and novelist Louise de Vilmorin, author of *Madame de.*
1967	*Antimémoires* is published and is an immediate best-seller.
1969	Louise de Vilmorin dies. Malraux continues to live at her family estate at Verrières.
1970	*Le Triangle noir* is published. De Gaulle dies.
1971	*Les Chênes qu'on abat.*
1973	Exhibition at the Fondation Maeght in Saint-Paul de Vence displays the works of Malraux's imaginary museum.
1974	*Lazare, La Tête d'obsidienne,* and *L'Irréel.*
1975	*Hôtes de passage.*
1976	*La Corde et les souris* and *L'Intemporel* published. Malraux dies of a pulmonary embolism on November 23. He is buried in a private ceremony at Verrières-le-Buisson. National homage at the Louvre. Memorial mass at Saint-Louis des Invalides, homily preached by R. P. Bockel.
1977	*Le Surnaturel* and *L'Homme précaire et la littérature* published posthumously.

Contributors

HAROLD BLOOM, Sterling Professor of the Humanities at Yale University, is the author of *The Anxiety of Influence, Poetry and Repression,* and many other volumes of literary criticism. His forthcoming study, *Freud: Transference and Authority,* attempts a full-scale reading of all of Freud's major writings. A MacArthur Prize Fellow, he is general editor of five series of literary criticism published by Chelsea House. During 1987–88, he was appointed Charles Eliot Norton Professor of Poetry at Harvard University.

GEOFFREY H. HARTMAN is Karl Young Professor of English and Comparative Literature at Yale. His books include *Wordsworth's Poetry* and *Saving the Text,* a study of Jacques Derrida.

DAVID WILKINSON is the author of *Malraux: An Essay in Political Criticism.*

LUCIEN GOLDMANN was the author of many works of philosophy, political theory and literary criticism. Among them are *Le Dieu Caché, Immanuel Kant,* and *The Philosophy of Enlightenment.*

C. J. GRESHOFF teaches at the University of Capetown in South Africa.

LEROY C. BREUNIG has taught at Cornell and Harvard Universities, and at Barnard College. He is the author of books and articles on Apollinaire as well as on the relationship between poetry and painting. He is also a member of the advisory board of the New York Literary Forum.

DEREK W. ALLAN teaches at Canberra University, Australia.

W. M. FROHOCK is Professor Emeritus of French at Harvard University and is a fellow of the Comargo Foundation in Cassis, France. He is the author of *André Malraux and the Tragic Imagination* and several shorter works on Malraux, as well as studies on French and American literature.

ROGER DIAL has written extensively on André Malraux and is Professor of French at Dalhousie University in Canada.

Bibliography

Alberes, R. M. *La Révolte des écrivains d'aujourd'hui*. Paris: Correa, 1949.

Allan, Derek W. "The Psychology of a Terrorist: Tchen in *La Condition humaine*." *Nottingham French Studies* 21 (May 1982): 48–66.

Astier, Emmanuel d'. *Portraits*. Paris: Gallimard, 1963.

Baumgartner, P. "Solitude and Involvement: Two Aspects of Tragedy in Malraux's Novels." *The French Review* (1965): 766–76.

Bevan, David. "André Malraux: Féministe." *Atlantis*, no. 7 (1982): 117–20.

Blend, C. D. *André Malraux: Tragic Humanist*. Columbus: Ohio State University Press, 1963.

———. "Early Expression of Malraux's Art Theory." *The Romanic Review* 53, no. 3 (1962): 199–213.

Blumenthal, Gerda. *André Malraux: The Conquest of Dread*. Baltimore: Johns Hopkins University Press, 1960.

Boak, C. D. "Jean Hougron and *La nuit indochinoise*." *France–Asie*, no. 174 (July–August 1962): 489–501.

———. "Malraux—A Note on Editions." *AUMLA*, no. 21 (May 1964): 79–83.

———. "Malraux and T. E. Lawrence." *The Modern Language Review* 61 (1966): 218–24.

Boak, Denis. *André Malraux*. Oxford: Clarendon, 1968.

Bree, Germaine, and Margaret Guiton. *An Age of Fiction*. New Brunswick, N. J.: Rutgers University Press, 1957.

Brombert, Victor. *The Intellectual Hero: Studies in the French Novel 1880–1955*. Philadelphia: Lippincott, 1961.

Burgum, Edwin Berry. *The Novel and the World's Dilemma*. Oxford: Oxford University Press, 1947.

Buroca, C. "Reflexions sur l'art chez Camus et chez Malraux." *Simoun*, no. 1 (January 1952): 116–20.

Casey, B. "André Malraux's *Heart of Darkness*." *Twentieth Century Literature* 5, no. 1 (1959): 21–26.

Caute, David. *Communism and the French Intellectuals*. New York: Macmillan, 1964.

Cazenave, Michel. *André Malraux*. Paris: L'Herne, 1982.

Chase, Richard V. *The Quest for Myth*. New Orleans: Louisiana State University Press, 1949.

Chevalier, H. M. "André Malraux: The Legend and the Man." *Modern Language Quarterly* 14 (1953): 199–208.

Chiaromonte, Nicola. "Malraux and the Demons of Action." *Partisan Review* 15 (1948): 776–89.

Clouard, H. "Itinéraire d'André Malraux." *Revue de Paris* 59 (December 1958): 82–95.

Cordle, T. H. "Malraux and Nietzsche's *Birth of Tragedy*." *Bucknell Review* 8, no. 2 (1959): 89–104.

Cornick, Martyn. "Malraux and Conrad: Imagery of Confrontation in *La Voie royale* and *Heart of Darkness*." *Mélanges Malraux Miscellany*, no. 15 (1983): 7–15.

Daniels, G. "The Sense of the Past in the Novels of André Malraux." In L. J. Austin et al., *Studies in Modern French Literature Presented to P. Mansel Jones*, 71–86. Manchester: Manchester University Press, 1961.

Drieu la Rochelle, Pierre. "Malraux, the New Man." In *From the N.R.F.—An Image of the Twentieth Century from the Pages of the Nouvelle Revue Française*, edited by Justin O'Brien. New York: Farrar, Straus & Cudahy, 1958.

Ehrenberg, Ilya. *Memoirs 1921–1941*. Translated by Tatania Shebunina and Yvonne Kapp. New York: World Publishing, 1964.

Ellis, L. B. "Some Existentialist Concepts in Gide, Malraux and Saint-Exupéry." *Bucknell Review* 10, no. 2 (1961): 164–73.

Erikson, E. H. "Identity and the Life Cycle." *Psychological Issues* 1, no. 1 (1959): Monograph I.

Fischer, Louis. *Men and Politics—An Autobiography*. New York: Duelle, Sloan & Pearce, 1941.

Flanner, Janet. *Men and Monuments*. New York: Harper & Row, 1957.

———. *Paris Journal 1944–1965*. New York: Atheneum, 1965.

Frank, Joseph. *The Widening Gyre*. New Brunswick, N.J.: Rutgers University Press, 1963.

Frohock, W. M. *André Malraux*. New York: Columbia University Press, 1974.

———. *André Malraux and the Tragic Imagination*. Stanford: Stanford University Press, 1951.

———. "Note for a Malraux Bibliography." *MLN* 65 (1950): 392–95.

———. "Notes on Malraux's Symbols." *The Romanic Review* 42 (1951): 274–81.

———. *Style and Temper; Studies in French Fiction 1925–1960*. Cambridge: Harvard University Press, 1967.

Gannon, Edward. *The Honor of Being a Man*. Chicago: Loyola University Press, 1957.

Garaudy, Roger. *Literature from the Graveyard: J. P. Sartre, F. Mauriac, A. Malraux, A. Koestler*. Translated by Joseph Bernstein. New York: International Publishers, 1948.

Gide, André. *Journal 1889–1939*. Paris: Bibliothèque de la Pléiade, 1959.

———. *Journal 1939–1949*. Paris: Bibliothèque de la Pléiade, 1959.

Gidley, Mick. "Malraux and the Attractions of Rhetoric in Faulkner's Later Public Comments." *William Faulkner*, no. 6 (May 1984): 20–35.

Goldberger, Avriel. *Visions of a New Hero; The Heroic Life According to André Malraux and Earlier Advocates of Human Grandeur*. Paris: Minard, 1965.

Greenlee, James W. *Malraux's Heroes and History*. De Kalb: Northern Illinois University Press, 1975.

Halda, Bernard. *Berenson et Malraux*. Paris: Minard, 1964.

Healey, Cathleen. "The Workings of Christianity in André Malraux's Fiction." *Studies*, no. 68 (1979): 92–108.

Hewitt, James. *André Malraux*. New York: Ungar, 1978.

Horvath, Violet. *André Malraux: The Human Adventure*. New York: New York University Press, 1969.

Jarrell, Randall. *A Sad Heart at the Supermarket: Essays and Fables*. New York: Atheneum, 1962.

Jenkins, Cecil. *André Malraux*. New York: Twayne, 1972.

Knapp, Bettina. "Archetypal Saturn/Chronos and the Goya/Malraux Dynamics." *Kentucky Romance Quarterly* 4 (1983): 373–87.

Knight, Everett W. *Literature Considered as Philosophy: The French Example*. New York: Macmillan, 1958.

Langlois, Walter G. *André Malraux: The Indochina Adventure*. New York: Praeger, 1966.

———. "Young Malraux and Eroticism: An Unpublished Chapter from *La Voie royale*." *Mélanges Malraux Miscellany*, no. 15 (1983): 32–42.

Lewis, R. W. B., ed. *André Malraux—A Collection of Critical Essays*. Englewood Cliffs, N.J.: Prentice-Hall, 1964.

Merleau-Ponty, Maurice. *Signs*. Translated by Richard C. McCleary. Illinois: Northwestern University Press, 1964.

Montalbetti, Jean. "La Vision dostoïevskienne d'André Malraux." *Nouvelle Revue Française* 59, no. 350 (March 1982): 79–87.

Morrisey, Will. *Reflections on Malraux: Cultural Founding in Modernity*. Lanham, Md.: University Press of America, 1984.

Peyre, Henri. *French Novelists of Today*. New York: Oxford University Press, 1967.

Reck, Rima Drell. *Literature and Responsibility: The French Novelist in the Twentieth Century*. Baton Rouge: Louisiana State University Press, 1969.

Regler, Gustav. *The Owl of Minerva*. Translated by Norman Denny. New York: Farrar, Straus & Cudahy, 1960.

Riffaterre, Michael. *Essais de stylistique structurale*. Paris: Flammarion, 1971.

Righter, William. *The Rhetorical Hero—An Essay on the Aesthetics of André Malraux*. London: Routledge & Kegan Paul, 1964. New York: Chilmark Press, 1964.

Savage, Catherine. *Malraux, Sartre and Aragon as Political Novelists*. University of Florida Monographs, no. 17. Gainesville: University of Florida, 1964.

Scheinman, Marc. "Trotsky and Malraux: The Political Imagination." In *The Artist and Political Vision*, edited by Benjamin Barber and Michael J. McGrath. New Brunswick, N.J.: Transaction, 1982.

Smith, Roch C. "Tchen's Sacred Isolation: Prelude to Malraux's Fraternal Humanism." *Studies in Twentieth Century Literature* 7 (1982): 45–57.

Soulsby, Sarah E. "Political Commitment as a Means of Revolt against Destiny as Seen in Some of André Malraux's Earlier Novels." *Journal of English*, no. 2 (1976): 95–109.

Sulzberger, Cyrus L. *A Long Row of Candles: Memoirs and Diaries 1934–1954*. New York: Macmillan, 1969.

Tarica, Ralph. "Ironic Figures in Malraux's Novels." In *Image and Theme—Studies in Modern French Fiction*, edited by W. M. Frohock. Cambridge: Harvard University Press, 1969.

Vivas, E. *The Artistic Transaction*. Columbus: Ohio State University Press, 1963.

Wilbur, C. M., and Julie L. Y. How. *Documents on Communism, Nationalism, and Soviet Advisers in China 1918–1927*. New York: Columbia University Press, 1956.

Williams, W. D. *Nietzsche and the French*. Oxford: Oxford University Press, 1952.

Wilson, Edmund. *The Bit between My Teeth*. New York: Farrar, Straus, 1966.

———. *The Shores of Light*. New York: Farrar, Straus, 1952.

Acknowledgments

" 'The Silence of the Infinite Spaces' " (originally entitled "In Search of Man") by Geoffrey H. Hartman from *André Malraux* by Geoffrey H. Hartman, © 1960 by Geoffrey H. Hartman. Reprinted by permission.

"The Bolshevik Hero" by David Wilkinson from *Malraux: An Essay in Political Criticism* by David Wilkinson, © 1967 by the President and Fellows of Harvard College. Reprinted by permission of Harvard University Press.

"The Structure of *La Condition humaine*" (originally entitled "Introduction to a Structural Study of Malraux's Novels") by Lucien Goldmann from *Towards a Sociology of the Novel* by Lucien Goldmann, © 1964 by Editions Gallimard, © 1975 by Tavistock Publications. Reprinted by permission of Tavistock Publications.

"Kyo and 'La Fraternité Virile' " (originally entitled "La Condition humaine") by C. J. Greshoff from *An Introduction to the Novels of André Malraux* by C. J. Greshoff, © 1975 by C. J. Greshoff. Reprinted by permission of A. A. Balkema, Rotterdam, Netherlands.

"Malraux's *Storm in Shanghai*" by LeRoy C. Breunig from *André Malraux: Metamorphosis and Imagination*, edited by Françoise Dorenlot and Micheline Tison-Braun, © 1979 by New York Literary Forum. Reprinted by permission of New York Literary Forum.

"André Malraux: The Commitment to Action in *La Condition humaine*" by Derek W. Allan from *French Forum* 6, no. 1 (January 1981), © 1981 by French Forum Publishers, Inc. Reprinted by permission.

"Gisors and the Human Condition" by W. M. Frohock from *Mélanges Malraux Miscellany* 14, no. 2 (Autumn 1982), © 1982 by Walter G. Langlois. Reprinted by permission.

"André Malraux on Revolution: Elements in *The Conquerors* and *Man's Fate*" by Roger Dial from *Mélanges Malraux Miscellany* 14, no. 1 (Spring 1982), © 1982 by Walter G. Langlois. Reprinted by permission.

Index

131